Manatees
and Dugongs
of the World

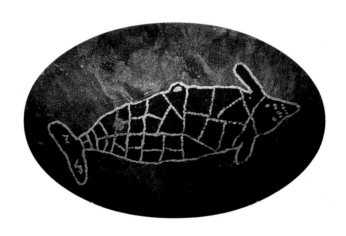

Text by Jeff Ripple
Photography by Doug Perrine

*W*orldLife
Discovery Guides

VOYAGEUR PRESS

Dedication

For my grandmother, Neva Ripple, who always believed in me

—Jeff Ripple

Edited by Danielle J. Ibister
Designed by Kristy Tucker
Printed in Hong Kong

First hardcover edition
99   00   01   02   03   5   4   3   2   1

First softcover edition
04   05   06   5   4   3   2

Library of Congress Cataloging-in-Publication Data available

ISBN 0-89658-393-7 (hardcover)
ISBN 0-89658-528-X (softcover)

Distributed in Canada by Raincoast Books, 9050 Shaughnessy Street, Vancouver, B.C. V6P 6E5

Published by Voyageur Press, Inc.
123 North Second Street, P.O. Box 338, Stillwater, MN 55082 U.S.A.
651-430-2210, fax 651-430-2211
books@voyageurpress.com
www.voyageurpress.com

Educators, fundraisers, premium and gift buyers, publicists, and marketing managers: Looking for creative products and new sales ideas? Voyageur Press books are available at special discounts when purchased in quantities, and special editions can be created to your specifications. For details contact the marketing department at 800-888-9653.

P A G E   1 : *A Florida manatee, near Crystal River, Florida.*
P A G E S   2 — 3 : *A Florida manatee rises to the surface to breathe in a spring near Crystal River, Florida.*
P A G E   3   I N S E T : *Aboriginal rock art portrays a dugong on a cave ceiling in northern Queensland, Australia. Photograph © Ben Cropp Productions/Innerspace Visions.*
P A G E   5 : *A Florida manatee in a spring near Crystal River squeezes its eyes shut, possibly for a nap or to ignore the photographer.*

Contents

Foreword

By Judith Vallee, Executive Director, Save the Manatee Club

SAVING MANATEES IS no easy task. When I first became interested in manatees in 1983 as a volunteer, I had no idea what was in store for me. I thought all the manatee's problems could be fixed by educating the public and by regulating boat speeds. I reasoned that if our elected officials and the public were apprised of the problem—that on average one out of every four manatees reported dead each year is killed by a boat—they would be motivated to do something. I didn't yet understand that education and boating restrictions are only temporary solutions unless habitat is also protected, because manatees, like all other beings on earth, need places to live.

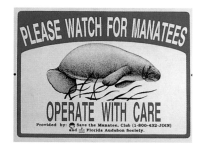

Are there answers? Maybe. If we care enough, if we are passionate enough to speak out for the manatee, if we are forever vigilant, manatees may have a chance. We must continue to educate all of Florida's citizens and visitors about manatees and the behaviors that endanger their existence. But make no mistake. Education alone is not the answer. We must also regulate. And as more people flock to develop manatee habitat and as the number of boats increases, so does the need for additional regulations increase exponentially.

Sanctuaries where no motorboats are allowed must be set aside throughout the manatee's range in Florida. Further, the pollution of our waterways must be prevented to protect manatees' food sources, and their winter refuges must be safeguarded to ensure adequate warm water will sustain the population. We need more enforcement officers on the water, and we are going to have to limit both the quantity and speed of boats using Florida's waterways. It is time for our elected officials and decision-makers to find the intestinal fortitude to make tough decisions.

How much are we willing to give up to save a manatee's life? Manatees work hard to survive in an environment that has been altered by an avalanche of human population growth. Is it too much to begin thinking seriously about our state's carrying capacity and resources? Is it too much to curb coastal development in manatee habitat? Is it too much to just slow down through manatee habitat, even if it takes a little longer to get where we are going?

My answer is unequivocal. It was once a T-shirt slogan: "I don't want to live in a world without manatees." Do you?

A Florida manatee is mirrored by its reflection at the surface of a Florida spring.

Author's Preface

Heeding the Siren's Call

I ENCOUNTERED MY first manatee in Florida's Ten Thousand Islands in Everglades National Park nearly 10 years ago. Canoeing alone on the Turner River, I was startled by a loud exhalation and stubby, bewhiskered snout, followed by nearly 13 feet of tubby, paddle-tailed mammal that rose to the surface and lingered beside my 14-foot canoe. The manatee was close enough to photograph and even touch, but I did neither, mesmerized by the sudden appearance of such an unlikely-looking creature. After a minute or two, it sank beneath the reddish water of the Turner, surfaced briefly to breathe about 200 feet away, and then I did not see it again. In the ensuing years, I've seen many more manatees and, during the research for this book, finally donned wet suit, mask, and snorkel to encounter them in their own element at Crystal River National Wildlife Refuge. They are no less improbable-looking underwater, but endearing just the same.

Manatees and their Indo-Pacific relatives, dugongs, are in grave danger of extinction due primarily to human activities. These animals are loved by millions of people and are increasingly popular tourist attractions, but most people have never seen one and know nothing about their life histories, the intriguing legends and traditions that surround them, the dangers they face each day, and what must be done to protect them and their habitat. *Manatees and Dugongs of the World* offers a broad introduction to manatees and dugongs. Hopefully, it will entice readers to explore further the fascinating lives of these aquatic mammals and to learn about what can be done—individually and collectively—to ensure their survival.

A number of people and organizations assisted me in gathering the information I needed to write the text for *Manatees and Dugongs of the World*, and I would like to take this opportunity to thank them: The staff and scientists at The Sirenia Project, particularly Karen Ausley and Bob Bonde; Sea World of Florida; U.S. Fish and Wildlife Service; University of Florida; Dr. Bruce Ackerman, Florida Marine Research Institute; Nancy Sadusky and Patti Thomson, Save the Manatee Club; Susan Dougherty, Art Yerian, and Dr. Mark Lowe, Homosassa Springs State Wildlife Park; and the staff and biologists of the Crystal River National Wildlife Refuge. Daryl Domning's *Bibliography and Index of the Sirenia and Desmostylia* has been an invaluable reference resource, and my text would have suffered without it. I am indebted to Drs. Helene Marsh, Dan Odell, Daryl Domning, and Mr. Bob Bonde for graciously agreeing to review drafts of the manuscript. Thanks also to Doug Perrine and Lisa Tun-Diaz, and of course, to my lovely wife Renée, for friendship and support. Any errors of fact in *Manatees and Dugongs of the World* are due to my misinterpretation of published research and information recounted to me, and I apologize for them in advance.

A juvenile crevalle jack shelters under a Florida manatee, Crystal River.

Photographer's Preface

WHILE WILDLIFE PHOTOGRAPHY can be a lonely pursuit, requiring long hours of solitude in the field, it is rarely accomplished by the efforts of one person alone. In creating the photographs displayed on these pages, taken over a 16-year period, I have had the invaluable assistance of numerous good-willed people. I hope those persons who I will inevitably neglect to mention in the following list will forgive the oversight. My thanks then to (in no particular order): Jim Reid, Bob Bonde, Dan Odell, Galen Rathbun, Frank Murru, Danny Paul, Wayne Hartley, Phil Courter and family, Sharon Alberdi and family, Tasso Welawo, Sandy Ben, Paul Parras, Linda Goodman, Tony Preen, Paul Anderson, Helene Marsh, Craig and Jesse Shankland, June Hunt and family, George McCotter, Susan Dougherty, Tom Linley, Shane Moore, Jesse White, Howard Hall, Bob Friel, Betsy Dearth, the Sirenia Project, Save the Manatee Club, American Pro Diving, SeaWorld of Florida, Homosassa Springs State Wildlife Park, C.A.L.M., Blue Springs State Park.

Many of the manatee photographs were taken in the waters around Crystal River, Florida, a town that has experienced great changes and tremendous growth over the last two decades. Due to the efforts of the Nature Conservancy, the State of Florida, and the federal government, much critical manatee habitat in this area has been protected, but parts remain vulnerable. As this book goes to press, the "Three Sisters Spring"—the actual site where many of these pictures were taken—is for sale, and may end up in the hands of developers. To urge the State of Florida to purchase and conserve this property and other properties adjoining manatee habitat, readers can contact the Florida Conservation and Recreational Lands Office by writing to 3900 Commonwealth Blvd., Mail Station 140, Tallahassee, FL 32399, or by calling (850) 487-1750, or contact the Save the Manatee Club at (800) 432-5646 for an update and to find out what needs to be done. Much of the federal effort to protect manatees is mandated by the Endangered Species Act, which needs to be reauthorized every few years. We should all appeal to our senators and representatives to resist any efforts to weaken this vital legislation.

Though development has been halted on certain parcels, the manatee's environment continues to change rapidly, as a result of our collective presence. Water quality is affected by the runoff from lawns, golf courses, septic tanks, farms and dairies, and so on. Spring flow is reduced by the pumping of water for a myriad of human needs. Aquatic plants imported from other areas choke out native vegetation and decompose into layers of anoxic muck. The greatest threat to sirenians used to be direct hunting by humans. Now that threat is greatly reduced, but they are in greater danger than ever before, simply because their environment is being destroyed by the ever-encroaching presence of humans. We strike them accidentally with our boats. The seagrass beds they feed upon are destroyed by pollution from urban and agricultural sources, and by fishing trawlers. They suffer mass mortalities due to red tides, which appear to be increasing in frequency, possibly due to excess nutrients running down our rivers from both agricultural and urban

A Florida manatee cruises its tank at SeaWorld of Florida.

sources.

If manatees and dugongs are to survive, we must not only act directly by protecting them and their environment, but also indirectly by limiting our own numbers. Sirenians and other wildlife simply cannot cope with the changes accumulating as a result of the ever-expanding human population. Every three days the human population of Florida increases by a number equal to the total number of Florida manatees in existence. We can ensure that our grandchildren will be able to see manatees and dugongs only if we have fewer grandchildren.

$\mathcal{A}$ First Glimpse

LEFT: *A Florida manatee is backlit
by sun rays in the clear waters of Homosassa Springs, Florida.*
ABOVE: *An Antillean manatee feeds on seagrass
(Thalassia testudinum) in the Caribbean Sea
off the coast of Belize.*

TENDRILS OF FOG rose slowly from the placid, crystalline window of Three Sisters Spring and climbed through a tangle of shoreline trees before escaping into the blue December sky. The water stirred and parted as a pair of nostrils broke the surface, snuffed like a person breathing through a snorkel, and then slipped below again. These nostrils were followed by another pair, and then three or four more pairs rose together, blowed, and sank from sight. Manatees had entered the spring from the Crystal River, seeking its warm, sweet water and the unbroken silence of dawn. Below the surface, a mother manatee nursed her calf, rolling slightly to one side to allow the calf a better grip on the nipple beneath her left flipper. The calf suckled eagerly for a couple of minutes, and then both mother and calf broke the surface to breathe.

By this time, more than fifteen manatees occupied the spring, in various stages of repose. Some clustered near a log, flippers wedged into the sandy bottom, asleep. Occasionally one would rise as if levitating, breathe, and then descend in the same, trance-like state. A couple of manatees scratched their backs vigorously against another submerged log. Another investigated the limestone confines of the spring, nibbling vegetation from an overhanging bush. It arced backward, did a couple of lazy barrel rolls, and moved toward the narrow run that led to the river.

This describes manatee life at its most idyllic. Unfortunately, they rarely enjoy such moments of peace, particularly during the day, when curious swimmers and boaters crowd around, anxious to have a "manatee experience." Three Sisters Spring and others in the Crystal River are critical sanctuaries for many of the fewer than 3,000 manatees that survive in Florida. Manatee populations have been eliminated or significantly reduced in many areas of western Africa, the Caribbean, and the Amazon River Basin. Dugongs, a close relative of manatees, are now rare along coastal countries around the Indian Ocean and elsewhere throughout their range; they are only relatively abundant in the coastal waters of northern Australia. In some places, they have disappeared completely, as did the Steller's sea cow, a gigantic sirenian nearly 30 feet (9.1 m) long that lived in the frigid waters of the Bering Sea. This grand animal was overhunted to extinction less than thirty years after Georg Steller brought it to Europe's attention in the eighteenth century. Manatees and dugongs have few predators other than humans, and only humans can be held accountable for the current predicament of these ancient aquatic mammals. This book is devoted to helping people better understand manatees and dugongs, and to improving the relationship between humans and sirenians in this fragile world.

Taxonomy and Relationship to Other Mammals

Manatees and dugongs, commonly described as "sea cows," belong to the taxonomic order Sirenia (named after the sirens of Homeric legend) and are collectively referred to as "sirenians." Within the order Sirenia are two families containing four living species. Family Trichechidae consists of the West Indian (including Florida and Antillean subspecies), the Amazonian, and the West African manatees. Family Dugongidae includes the dugong and the recently extinct Steller's sea cow.

Sirenians are not noted for their attractiveness, despite being named for the infamously beautiful Greek sirens whose rapturous voices lured many a sailor to a shipwreck death. One English scientist,

A dugong, accompanied by golden pilot jacks, feeds on sea grass (Halophila ovalis) off the coast of Australia.

A manatee appears to balance on its tail in the clear waters of Three Sisters Spring near Crystal River, Florida.

Several manatees rest undisturbed near the bottom of a spring near Crystal River, Florida.

upon seeing a West African manatee in the wild for the first time, commented, "Floating idly just below the surface of the water, maybe munching a water lily stem, the manatee looks to me disarmingly like a cross between a dirty barrage balloon and a gray maggot." Most people find them endearingly homely. All sirenians have large, streamlined, spindle- or cigar-shaped bodies with no externally apparent neck; flippers; and a large, flattened tail for locomotion. In manatees the tail is shaped like a wide, flat paddle, while dugongs have a fluked tail like whales and dolphins. All sirenians have a sparse covering of hair over their bodies. Sirenian bones are thick and solid and heavy, and the small cranial cavity houses a brain many scientists consider rather small for such a large animal. Despite the manatee's small brain, however, many scientists consider them quite intelligent. All extant sirenians have teeth, and all species have horny plates in the mouth to help crush fibrous aquatic vegetation. Despite the mythical allure of the siren's song, sirenians use only a small repertoire of squeaks and chirps; some scientists suspect that manatees, like elephants, may also communicate via infrasonic sounds indiscernible to human ears.

Sirenians are marine mammals, as are whales, dolphins, seals, sea lions, walruses, sea otters, and polar bears. Like all mammals, they breathe air through lungs, possess hair, give birth to live young, and produce milk for their young. On a superficial level, they most closely resemble cetaceans (whales and dolphins) and pinnipeds (seals, sea lions, and walruses), with whom they share a similar body shape. Like these animals, sirenians are physiologically adapted to life in the water, possess vestigial remnants (such as finger bones and pelvic structures) that hearken back to their ancient life as land dwellers, and depend on aquatic habitat for survival. In fact, as recently as the nineteenth century, scientists incorrectly surmised manatees to be strange,

The Order of Sirenia

Family Trichechidae
West Indian manatee (*Trichechus manatus*)
Florida subspecies (*T. manatus latirostris*)
Antillean subspecies (*T. manatus manatus*)
Amazonian manatee (*Trichechus inunguis*)
West African manatee (*Trichechus senegalensis*)
Family Dugongidae
Dugong (*Dugong dugon*)
Steller's Sea Cow (*Hydrodamalis gigas*)

tropical forms of the walrus and placed both animals in the same family.

Despite these similarities, manatees and dugongs bear no evolutionary kinship with any other groups of living marine mammals. Their closest living relatives are elephants and, unlikely as it may seem, they are distantly related to hyraxes (small, furry, rodent-like creatures) and aardvarks. Sirenians share with these animals certain proteins that suggest a common ancestry, as well as similar dental characteristics, lack of a collarbone, and toenails or hooves rather than claws. Sirenians are also closely related to an extinct group of marine mammals called desmostylians, which were hippo-like herbivores that lived during the Oligocene and Miocene epochs, roughly five million to thirty-five million years ago.

Sirenian Evolution

Much of what we know about the evolution of sirenians is the result of fossil studies by Dr. Daryl Domning of Howard University and his colleagues. The following evolutionary information is based largely on his findings. Sirenians probably first appeared some fifty million years ago during the early Eocene epoch. Although the oldest known fossils come from Jamaica, most scientists think sirenians evolved in the Old World—Eurasia and Africa—and within a few million years proliferated into several different genera, all as completely aquatic as modern manatees and dugongs but somewhat different in appearance. Most known fossil remains belong to a diverse group of ancient dugong-like creatures called dugongids, which were distributed along coastlines worldwide (including in the Caribbean, where only manatees are found now). Dugongid fossil remains dating back to the Middle Eocene have been found in marine deposits (areas of sedimentary rock once covered by water) from Spain to Egypt, western Europe, the southeastern United States, the Caribbean, South America, the North

Pacific, and the Indian Ocean. Dugongids reached their peak in abundance and diversity during the Miocene epoch five to twenty-five million years ago, when tropical conditions held sway over much of the planet. The most widespread genus at the time, *Metaxytherium*, was likely the forefather of a more recent subfamily of dugongids that included the Steller's sea cow.

South America is considered the ancestral home of manatees (trichechids), descendants of ancient sirenians that reached the South American continent, perhaps during the Eocene, and subsequently became genetically isolated from other sirenians over several million years. Evidence of the earliest known trichechid, *Potamosiren*, came from Middle Miocene fossil deposits in Colombia. Early manatees were probably confined to coastal rivers and estuaries in South America, feeding on freshwater vegetation, while dugongids grazed seagrass meadows in the Caribbean, western Atlantic, and elsewhere. Geologic events during the Late Miocene closed the Pacific entrance to the upper Amazon River, temporarily isolating manatees in the Amazon basin. These animals, which adapted to consume the floating meadows of vegetation on Amazon lakes, eventually became the Amazonian manatee.

One of the principal features that separates manatees from dugongs is their dentition, or teeth.

A Florida manatee calf nurses from its mother.

Manatees have a large number of small molars that fall out when worn, and are replaced by others further back in the mouth. Extinct dugongs had fewer teeth and, in some cases, large, bladelike tusks, which they used to uproot the nutritious rhizomes, or underground stems, of seagrass. (Modern dugongs do not use their tusks, except perhaps for fighting.) As the Andes formed, tremendous amounts of nutrients and silt were dumped into South American rivers, increasing the amount of aquatic vegetation, including nutritious, but abrasive, grasses. By the late Miocene or Pliocene, manatees evolved specialized teeth to take advantage of this abundant new food source. During the Pliocene, Indo-Pacific dugongs evolved ever-growing cheek teeth as continental glaciation lowered sea level and increased erosion and silt runoff into the seagrass meadows where dugongs fed. According to Daryl Domning, Caribbean dugongs, unlike manatees, may have failed to adapt their dentition to the new feeding conditions and therefore, over time, became extinct.

Today, only four species of sirenians remain, and only near the mouth of the Amazon do more than one species of manatee occur together. No one is certain what caused the decline in the diversity of sirenians, although some combination of changes in climate, quality, and variety of aquatic plants, and competition with other herbivores may be responsible.

Humans and Sirenians

Why are humans fascinated by manatees and dugongs? People are attracted to their rarity, their large size, and their gentle nature. Educational programs tell us sirenians are in danger of extinction and will survive only with our help. In Florida, people flock by the thousands to see manatees in aquariums and in warm-water springs where they gather during the winter. Wayward manatees, such as Chessie, who ventured into Chesapeake Bay at the wrong time of year and required rescue, attract wide-scale media attention and public empathy.

Historically, sirenians have been revered by humans in myth, in religious tradition, for their medicinal value, and as an important food source. In Indonesia the meat is believed to give strength,

A head-on view of a dugong.

ABOVE: *In this mural painted by Ely Kish,* Metaxytherium, *a small-tusked dugong, and her calf feed on sea grasses in the Caribbean Sea more than three million years ago. A variety of fishes, other marine mammals, and the ancient toothed whale* Basilosaurus *accompany them. Photograph © Chip Clark, The Smithsonian Institution*

RIGHT, ABOVE: *A skull of a fossil dugong* Metaxytherium floridanum *from the mid-Miocene (left) and skull of a modern manatee (right) from the Florida Museum of Natural History, Gainesville. Differences in the size of the skull, the downward angle of the rostrum, and the teeth are immediately apparent.*

RIGHT, BELOW: *A fossil dugong tusk (left) and molar (top) compared with a fossil manatee molar (bottom). Teeth are among the principal features that set apart manatees from dugongs.*

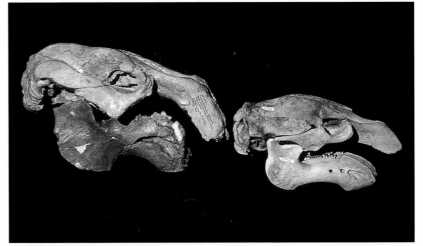

A manatee feeds on hydrilla, an exotic aquatic plant. Manatees have been used in many parts of the world, including Florida in the 1960s, to help clear aquatic weeds, with varying success.

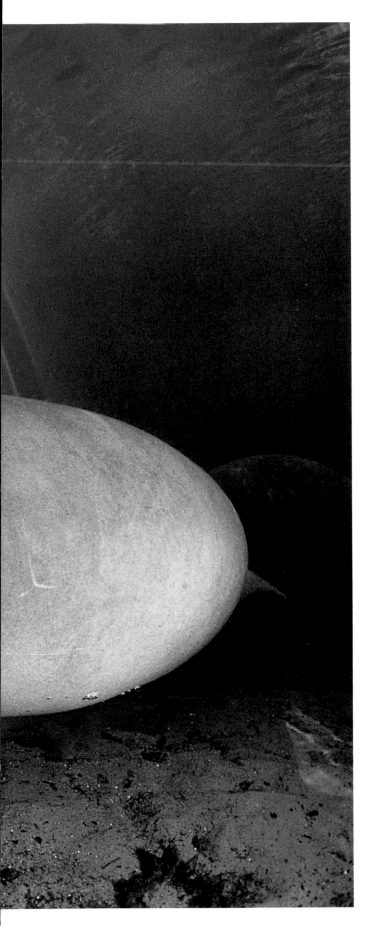

the fat is used in obstetrics and cooking, the siren's tears are a love potion, and the incisors are thought to render their owner invulnerable to harm. In many native cultures, manatees and dugongs figure prominently in legends that define cultural conduct. The Rama Indians of coastal Nicaragua believe that if a hunter fails to return a manatee's bones to where it was killed, he will be unable to find manatees on future hunts. Near the Stewart River on the Cape York Peninsula of northern Australia, the sandbeach natives used to believe that any dugong remains must be discarded into the river (rather than burned) to avoid horrible luck.

Many stories have been told to explain how manatees and dugongs came to be. The Kilenge people of the northwest coast of New Britain in Melanesia say that the dugong was originally a wild pig that underwent a transformation. A Lamu story holds that dugongs are the descendants of women who were lost at sea in ancient days. Classical authors gave the siren the attributes of a seductive girl, based on stories by sailors who fixated on the exposed genitals and teat under each flipper. As recently as 1971, fishermen in Zanzibar who captured a female dugong had to swear that they had not "interfered" with it.

Many native cultures that traditionally relied on sirenians as a food source are no longer permitted, or no longer find it feasible, to hunt these animals because they are so scarce. Others still hunt on a subsistence level, although that practice is limited to fewer places than in the past. Overhunting has caused sirenian declines in some areas, but manatees and dugongs are disappearing more often as a result of other human activities, including coastal development, dam construction, shoreline netting, and increased boating. A number of conservation groups and government agencies worldwide are working to produce programs and materials to educate people about manatees and dugongs and how we can share the world with them. (See Appendix III for addresses and phone numbers of organizations you can contact if you want to become involved in sirenian conservation.) Most countries have banned or severely limited the hunting of sirenians, although enforcement of these laws

Sun rays bathe a manatee with light in the shallow spring run of Blue Spring State Park, Florida.

varies widely among countries.

None of this is new. We have heard this same story connected with the histories of thousands of other life forms, some still with us, some not. But it boils down to this: We must become better citizens of our planet. If we cannot curb our own runaway population growth and conscientiously factor the survival needs of wildlife and the environment into our day-to-day actions, we stand no chance of saving manatees, dugongs, or any other species. In the long term, unless we step back from the notion that human needs come first, we will not even save ourselves.

Children observe a manatee through a glass window at Homosassa Springs State Wildlife Park, Florida.

Snorkelers interact with a manatee in the Crystal River National Wildlife Refuge, Florida.

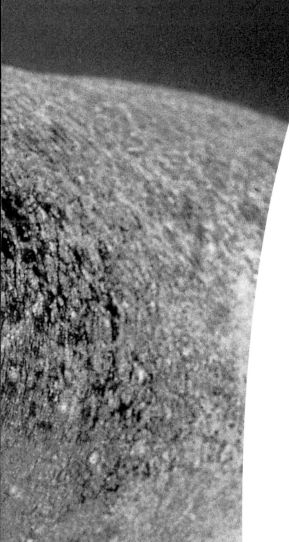

CHAPTER 2

Manatees

LEFT: *A Florida manatee in Crystal River, Florida.*
ABOVE: *A Florida manatee grazes on algae coating a
rock in a spring near Crystal River.*

MANATEES LIVE PRIMARILY in warm tropical and subtropical waters of the Americas and western Africa. There are three species—West Indian (*Trichechus manatus*), West African (*Trichechus senegalensis*), and Amazonian (*Trichechus inunguis*)—and all belong to the family Trichechidae. The West Indian manatee is further divided into two subspecies—the Florida (*Trichechus manatus latirostris*) and Antillean (*Trichechus manatus manatus*). All are rare and threatened with extinction.

There has been much discussion of the derivation of the word "manatee." "Manatee" comes from the Spanish word *manatí*; the conflict arises over the word from which *manatí* originates. It was believed to be derived from the Carib Indian (a cannibalistic West Indian tribe) word *manatui* (or a similar spelling), which is often reported to mean "big beaver." This belief was disputed in 1941 by George Gaylord Simpson, who suggested that *manatí* comes from a Carib word for "a woman's breast." This word differs slightly in various dialects, including *manati* (Arekuna), *manatë* (Makuche), *manate* (Galibi), and *manadu* (Akawai), among others. Simpson's suggestion is plausible because the small, wrinkled teats of female manatees are a distinguishing characteristic. Others credit the common name as a reference to the Spanish word *manos*, meaning "hands"—alluding to the manual dexterity of a manatee's foreflippers and possibly the presence of nails on some species' flippers.

The Florida Manatee

The Florida manatee (*Trichechus manatus latirostris*) is probably the only sirenian known to most North Americans. This subspecies appears on calendars and in books, and stars in the occasional documentary. An estimated 2,200 to 2,600 Florida manatees (based on 1997 survey results) live in the wild. A handful of aquariums have them on exhibit in various parts of the United States, primarily Florida and California. Still, many people do not know what a manatee is, what it looks like, or where it lives. Most Floridians have probably never seen this massive yet secretive animal in the wild.

Despite its discreet nature, and in large part because of its endangered status, the Florida manatee is the most studied sirenian in the world. Millions of dollars have been spent studying virtually every aspect of this animal, in captivity and in the wild, since the late 1960s. The Antillean and West African manatees share many traits with the Florida manatee in regards to anatomy, physiology, social behavior, reproductive behavior, and to some degree use of habitat. Studies of the Florida manatee, therefore, can often be applied to these animals as well.

The Florida manatee can be physically distinguished from the Antillean subspecies mainly by certain characteristics of the skull. Put them side by side in the flesh and even trained biologists may have difficulty telling them apart. Florida manatees live primarily in bays, estuaries, rivers, and coastal areas where seagrasses and other aquatic vegetation are abundant. They can live in and move freely between freshwater, brackish, and marine habitats, although scientists don't know how long they can remain in salt water before having to find a freshwater source. Manatees spend most of their time in water three to seven feet (1–2 m) deep, and avoid flats and shallows that are not adjacent to deeper water. They do, however, use high tides to reach feeding grounds, such as those on seagrass flats, that are too shallow during low tide. When traveling along the coast, manatees typically stay in water from ten to sixteen feet (3–5 m) deep, avoiding water more than twenty feet (6 m) deep and currents greater than three miles per hour.

Range

The range of Florida manatees varies somewhat depending on the season. Their historical range is thought to have centered in southern Florida, with small groups wintering in warm-water springs in northern Florida. During the last thirty years, loss of habitat in south Florida and the construction of several power plants in coastal central and northern Florida and Georgia have compelled more manatees to remain farther north during the winter than in the past. These power plants produce warm-water discharges in which manatees like to congregate. In general, Florida manatees are restricted to peninsular Florida north to southern Georgia. During the summer, however, they may range as far north as Rhode Island and as far west as Mississippi and Louisiana. There have been sightings of manatees at West End, Grand Bahama, about fifty miles (80 km) east of West Palm Beach, Florida. Most reports of manatees from

Virginia

N. Carolina

S. Carolina

Alabama

Georgia

Mississippi

Louisiana

Atlantic Ocean

Gulf of Mexico

Florida

Bahamas

● Year round range of the Florida manatee
● Seasonal range of the Florida manatee

southern Texas, northern Mexico, Bimini, and other southern Bahamian islands are probably Antillean manatees rather than far-ranging Florida manatees. Manatee sightings in Louisiana and Mississippi have increased as the population of Florida manatees in the Big Bend area of Florida has grown, while Texas sightings have decreased as the Mexican population of Antillean manatees has dwindled.

In the Gulf of Mexico, Florida manatees are rarely found more than half a mile from the mouth of a river, ranging along the coast from the Ten Thousand Islands in southwest Florida north to the Suwannee River throughout the year. These manatees typically spend their summers in estuaries and grassbeds in rivers. On the Atlantic Coast, manatees are found from the St. Johns River in northeastern Florida south to Miami and infrequently in the Florida Keys and Florida Bay. Manatees rarely cross Florida Bay between the Atlantic and Gulf coasts of Florida, so the two populations generally remain separate. The Indian River Lagoon in east-central Florida, especially the northern Banana River, is a critical feeding area year-round. As many as 245 manatees have been seen there during the spring and more than 100 during the summer. Warm-water effluents in Georgia also attract many manatees year-round.

Several dozen manatees have been tagged with radio or satellite transmitters by scientists to track their movements. Data from studies of tagged individuals have shown that most of their travel occurs seasonally as they move between favored winter and summer grounds. They generally travel alone or in small groups and can cover long distances. One tagged manatee traveled 528 miles (845 km) between Blue Spring in the St. Johns River to Coral Gables, south of Miami. Another traveled more than 143 miles (229 km) in four days from the Indian River to southern Georgia. Chessie, a tagged adult male manatee received extensive media and scientific attention after traveling more than 1,500 miles (2,500 km) from Florida to Rhode Island, breaking records for the longest migration by a West Indian manatee and the most northerly location for that species.

Florida manatees live primarily in bays, estuaries, rivers, and coastal areas where seagrasses and other aquatic vegetation are abundant.

ABOVE: *Two manatees nuzzle in Homosassa Springs, Florida.*
RIGHT: *Florida manatees gather in a Miami canal near a warm water discharge on a cold, winter morning.*

Winter Range

Some manatees live in the St. Johns River throughout the year, and they congregate at Blue Spring in Blue Spring State Park during cold winter weather. The number of manatees at Blue Spring has increased during the last fifteen years because some of the manatees have successfully raised calves and other manatees have migrated from other areas. Because northern Florida in winter is subject to sudden cold snaps—which can be fatal to manatees—most of the population migrates south during the winter. They congregate in warm-water discharges from coastal power plants, including Florida Power & Light's plants at Cape Canaveral, Port Everglades, Riviera Beach, and Fort Myers. Manatees have become accustomed to these warm-water refuges, and interruptions in the discharge from these plants could be devastating.

On the Gulf Coast, most wintering manatees congregate in the springs of the Crystal River and around coastal power plant discharges near Crystal River, at Tampa Bay, and in the Caloosahatchee River at Fort Myers. A few manatees linger during the winter months in large springs on the Suwannee River, including Manatee and Fanning springs.

Physical Description

The Florida manatee, like all sirenians, has what has been described as a "spindle-shaped" body. Adult females may reach a length of thirteen feet (3.9 m) and weigh more than 3,000 pounds (1,500 kg). An average adult manatee is about ten feet (3 m) long and weighs about 1,200 pounds (500 kg). Calves are dark at birth, but lighten to gray after about a month. As with all manatees, the tail is flat and rounded into a broad paddle. They have a pair of short, amazingly flexible, paddle-shaped front flippers, tipped with three to four fingernails. Although there are no apparent hind limbs, vestigial pelvic bones remain deep in the pelvic musculature.

The skin, textured much like a football and sparsely covered with hairs, ranges in color from gray to brown and may vary depending on what organisms—such as algae—are growing on it. The surface layer of skin constantly sloughs off, perhaps to reduce the buildup of algae, barnacles, and other growths. Beneath the skin is a layer of blubber less than an inch thick, and fat deposits occur among muscles and around the intestines.

On some manatees, the head looks much too

A Florida manatee, Homosassa Springs.

small for the rotund body. The face is round and wears a perpetually placid expression. The manatee has prominent whiskers, known as vibrissae, on the large, flexible, upper lip. Manatees use their lips and flippers to handle vegetation when feeding. The nostrils, located on the upper surface of the nose, are tightly closed by valves when the manatee submerges. A manatee's eyes are small and located on the sides of the head. Its ears, which lack external lobes, are visible only as tiny openings located just behind the eyes.

Scientists use a manatee's inner ear bones to estimate the animal's age once it has died, counting growth layers much as they would count the rings of a tree. A captive manatee at the Bradenton Museum in Florida is known to be more than 50 years old, and a manatee named Rosie at Homosassa Springs State Wildlife Park is estimated to be over 35 years old.

The Sensory Manatee

Manatees use all the senses familiar to humans to survive in their world, including sight, sound, touch, taste, and smell. The retina of a manatee's eye has both rods and cones, suggesting manatees can see in both dim and bright light, and they may be able to see colors; their eyesight is thought to be good.

Although manatees hear slight sounds, such as dripping water, from 160 feet (50 m) away, and cows respond to squealing calves more than 200 feet

(60 m) away, recent studies suggest manatees have difficulty hearing the frequency emitted by boat engines. Slow-moving boats appear to be especially difficult for manatees to hear, indicating that a manatee struck by a boat may simply not hear the engine in time to move out of danger. Still, manatees are renowned for their ability to detect sound among some South American tribes, and it is a great compliment when a person is said to "hear like a manatee." Some scientists think the manatee receives sound best not through the ear openings, but rather within a large area near the animal's cheekbones, which are in direct contact with the internal ear bones. Manatees, like elephants, may be able to produce and hear infrasonic frequencies, sounds too low to be detected by humans. While some marine mammals, such as cetaceans, use ultrasonic sounds for echolocation and navigation, manatees use their sounds solely for communication. Most of the sounds they make can be heard by humans.

Manatees communicate with chirps, whistles, and squeaks that presumably are produced with the larynx. They vocalize to maintain contact with each other, during play, or when they are frightened or sexually aroused. Scientists believe manatees can convey different information by varying the pitch, loudness, and duration of calls. Manatees may call often to maintain contact when traveling or feeding, particularly in murky water, and they appear to vocalize more rapidly when greeting new arrivals or when startled as a group and fleeing an area.

There has been little research regarding how well manatees can taste or smell. Manatees have taste buds on the back of the tongue, and scientists think they use chemoreception (physiological responses of a sense organ to chemical stimulus) to choose preferred foods and avoid eating noxious plants.

Scientists think that manatees may also communicate by touch, taste, or smell, because manatees are often observed touching and mouthing one another. Taste and smell may help manatees recognize one another. Males, as with many other mammals, may use taste and smell to determine if a female is in estrus. The short hairs scattered over the skin may heighten a manatee's ability to detect water movements caused by nearby manatees or the touch of other species.

Manatees seem to enjoy being touched. Females and calves maintain lots of body contact, and manatees are often seen nuzzling each other or scratching their bellies on rocks, submerged logs, or the bottom. While many manatees ignore swimmers and studiously avoid any contact with them, some manatees at Crystal River actively seek people out, having learned that swimmers never seem to tire of stroking them.

Manatee anatomy and physiology

Manatee bones are massive and heavy, and the ribs and long bones of the forelimbs lack marrow cavities. The heavy bones may act as ballast to offset the buoyancy caused by the manatee's large lungs, and by gas generated during the digestion process. Some scientists think the extreme density of the bones may be a result of the manatee's slow metabolic rate. Manatees are different from most other mammals (including dugongs) in that they have only six cervical vertebrae rather than seven.

Manatees' teeth are constantly being replaced. Grinding molars form at the back of the jaw and

A Florida manatee arrives from the ocean, its back covered with barnacles.

Barnacles festoon the tail of a Florida manatee, recently arrived from the ocean to a freshwater spring. Scars where others have fallen off after the manatee left salt water are also plainly visible. Algae frequently grows on manatees living in fresh water and is often grazed upon by mullet and sometimes other manatees.

A Florida manatee and her calf.

gradually move forward as front molars fall out. This tooth replacement mechanism is an adaptation to the manatee's diet of abrasive plants that are often mixed with sand. Wrinkles in the molars' surface enamel may also help reduce wear. The front teeth of Florida manatees often show extreme wear: this may be caused by the quartz sand substrates common on the Atlantic and Gulf coasts.

Manatees possess a digestive system much like that of horses, one adapted to digest high-fiber, low-protein vegetation. The cardiac gland, a large structure that protrudes from the stomach, coats swallowed food with mucus. This protects the lining of the digestive system from abrasive plant material as it moves through the digestive tract. Once food leaves the stomach, it passes to the intestines, which in an adult manatee can measure 130 feet (40 m) in length. The bulk of digestion occurs in the rear part of the gut, where intestinal bacteria break down cellulose from plant material. Food may take a week to move through the animal, and the slow digestive process produces copious quantities of methane gas.

Manatees are usually submerged when they feed and so must be able to hold their breath for long periods. Manatees breathe through two valved nostrils situated at the tip of the nose. They exhale at the surface and, like whales and dolphins, can renew about 90 percent of the air in their lungs in a single breath. (When at rest, humans ordinarily renew only about 10 percent of the air in their lungs with each breath). The manatee's lungs are flattened, about three feet (1 m) long, and situated along the back.

The shape, position, and internal structure of the lungs help manatees float horizontally in the water. By changing the volume of their lungs, they can hang motionless in the water column and move up or down with little effort. This ability, combined with their heavy bones, gives them excellent buoyancy control and allows them to feed efficiently them near the bottom.

When manatees dive, they hold their breath like humans. Manatees have been reported to stay submerged for up to 20 minutes, but scientists doubt they can dive beyond about 33 feet (10 m). The average time between breaths at rest is two to four minutes, and smaller manatees need to breathe more frequently than larger ones. During strenuous activity a manatee may need to take a breath every 30 seconds.

A manatee swims by flapping its tail and steering with its tail and flippers. Manatees can be quite acrobatic, doing barrel rolls, gliding on their back, performing somersaults, and standing on their head or tail. Their average cruising speed is about two to six miles (4–10 km) per hour, but they can reach speeds of more than 15 miles (25 km) per hour for short bursts.

Metabolism and susceptibility to cold

Manatees are extremely intolerant of cold water. Scientists believe this intolerance is due primarily to their low metabolic rate, which is only 15 to 22 percent that of a land mammal of similar body weight. A low metabolic rate benefits large tropical mammals because it allows them to stay cool in warm water and survive on a nutrient-poor diet. But Florida is on the northern edge of the West Indian manatee's range, and winter cold fronts that bring several consecutive mornings with lows at or near freezing can kill Florida manatees. Juvenile animals are particularly susceptible to cold weather mortality, because their smaller body size creates a greater potential for heat loss. Nursing infants are

A Florida manatee calf nurses from its mother.

virtually unaffected, perhaps because the rich milk from their mothers helps compensate for their small size and because their mothers take them to warm water when necessary.

Manatees spend less time eating during cold weather. They may quit eating altogether if water temperatures drop to near 50°F (10°C). Dead animals recovered by researchers after severe cold snaps generally have empty stomachs, have depleted their fat reserves, and show signs of dehydration. Several studies indicate that a manatee's layer of blubber may not provide sufficient insulation against cold water and that its metabolism may be unable to increase sufficiently to counteract the loss of body heat brought on by sudden cold. Forty-six Florida manatees are thought to have died from cold-related stress in 1989, and exposure to cold is blamed for many deaths in the winters of 1977, 1981, and 1984.

An adult manatee's normal body temperature hovers at about 97.5° F (36.4° C), but may vary seasonally or with water temperature. Manatees generally start looking for warm water when the air temperature drops below 50° F (10° C) or water

Like all marine mammals, sirenians need to surface to breathe air.

temperature dips to 68° F (20° C). During a typical year, most Florida manatees migrate to southern Florida or converge on springs and other warm-water sources throughout the state. This migration usually lasts from November through March. Some individuals move between warm-water refuges during the winter. Between cold fronts, most manatees make short feeding trips that last up to a week or more, from their refuges to feed. Other animals stay in coastal areas or bays where there is steady water temperature and a reliable food source, such as the shallow nearshore waters of Everglades National Park in extreme southern Florida.

Some studies indicate that manatees may acclimate to cold temperatures as winter progresses to spring. A study by Dr. Daniel Hartman in the late 1970s showed that when November air temperatures dropped to 50°F (10°C), manatees flocked into the Crystal River for warmth, but the air temperature had to plummet to near 41°F (5°C) to force the same manatees back into the river in March. Studies of wintering manatees at power plants demonstrated a similar pattern. Some scientists, however, argue that the lower temperature required to force manatees back to warm water late in the winter may reflect the manatee's increased need to feed rather than acclimation to cold weather. During the winter, a manatee's blubber layer shrinks as the animal taps into its energy reserves. It is therefore less willing in early spring to abandon food sources and rush back to warmer water.

Diet and Feeding

Manatees often spend more than eight hours a day feeding. In that time, they can consume nearly 10 percent of their body weight in wet vegetation. They are opportunistic herbivores, grabbing and tearing plants with their lips and then passing the material back to the molars for chewing. Florida manatees are known to eat more than sixty species of plants, preferring submerged vegetation over emergent, floating, and shoreline varieties. In fresh water, Florida manatees dine on a wide array of plants, including two invasive exotics—hydrilla and water hyacinth. At Blue Spring State Park, manatees were observed rooting for and devouring acorns that had fallen to the bottom from the live oaks

A Florida manatee resting on the bottom displays its flipper and elephant-like toenails.

overhanging the spring run. When necessary, manatees will even haul themselves partially out of the water to browse shoreline vegetation.

In salt water, a manatee's primary food is seagrass, including turtle grass, manatee grass, and shoal grass. Manatees have also been known to consume mangrove leaves and seedlings.

When feeding on seagrass, manatees crop the leaves. One report mentions manatees digging out the nutritious rhizomes of seagrass with their flippers, while others say manatees only eat rhizomes that are exposed by some other disturbance, such as strong currents. Their manner of feeding may depend largely on the species of seagrass being grazed. For example, small, tender species of seagrass are easily uprooted and consumed whole. Seagrasses of the genus *Thallasia*, on the other hand, are typically hard to dig up, so their rhizomes are rarely eaten. Although manatees frequently graze heavily on seagrass beds and occasionally eat exposed rhizomes, their feeding rarely makes a lasting impact on the seagrass community.

Manatees prefer to feed on the edges of seagrass beds, where they can escape to deeper water if disturbed. They also seek out protected water behind barrier islands, where they are sheltered from wind and currents. Wading birds, such as little blue herons and reddish egrets, often feed on small fish and invertebrates flushed out by grazing manatees.

Although manatees are primarily herbivores, they do consume small animals incidentally and opportunistically. A variety of invertebrates that cling to the leaves of mangroves or seagrass blades are unintentionally eaten; adding important protein to the manatees' diet. But there are instances of intentional carnivorism. Along the northern coast of Jamaica, fishermen complain that manatees suck the meat off the bones of fish caught in their gill nets, leaving the skeletons hanging in the mesh. Biologist Buddy Powell watched manatees in this area move from net to net as they looked for entangled fish. At Marineland of Florida, staff began feeding their manatees fish as a protein supplement after seeing manatees sucking the flesh off fish left by Amazonian dolphins sharing the tank. Biologist Sharon Tyson watched manatees in southeast Florida linger near fish-cleaning tables at the water's edge to claim the discarded remains of redfish, grouper, and flounder (while ignoring other kinds of fish). Tyson also observed one manatee catch a small flounder while feeding in thick seagrass. The manatee rose to the surface with the wriggling fish in its mouth and was about to swallow it when another manatee came along and tried to steal it. Perhaps the strangest manatee meal was reported by biologist Bob Bonde, who was observing manatees from a Brevard County dock when a dead rat floated out from under the dock and was quickly devoured by one of the manatees.

Social Behavior

Manatees are generally described by scientists as semi-social animals with relatively uncomplicated behavior. Scientists say that because manatees evolved in regions with warm temperatures, plentiful food, and few natural predators, these gentle mammals rarely needed work together to find food or shelter, or to defend themselves against enemies. They congregate at warm-water refuges during cold weather and occasionally feed in small groups at other times of the year, but these associations are

When a manatee breathes, only the tip of its snout protrudes above the water, which makes it difficult to see by boaters.

A B O V E : *Manatees "kissing" at Blue Spring State Park, Florida.*
L E F T : *A Florida manatee feeds on water hyacinth, another problem aquatic plant not native to Florida.*

A Florida manatee rests just below the surface of a spring, Crystal River, Florida.

The short hairs scattered over its skin may heighten a manatee's ability to detect water movements caused by nearby manatees or the touch of other animals, such as the crevalle jacks surrounding these manatees in Homosassa Springs, Florida.

temporary. The only strong, basic social relationship believed to exist between manatees is the bond between a female and her calf; the male manatee plays no role in rearing the calf. A calf is fully formed at birth and able to swim with its mother within a few moments of taking its first breath. It calls to its mother just after birth; this vocalization is thought to be part of the bonding process. It remains close to its mother's side, usually swimming directly behind her flipper. The calf relies solely on its mother for nutrition and guidance regarding feeding and resting areas, travel routes, and warm-water refuges. If a human or another manatee approaches the calf, the mother may position herself between the intruder and the calf, but she will not attack. If she feels threatened or senses danger in any way, she and her calf will flee, calling to each other as they swim away.

The bond between a mother and calf is strong. In one instance, a manatee cow and her calf were separated by a closed floodgate for several hours and constantly called back and forth until the gate was raised. When a cow and calf are trapped in an unsafe area, rescuers frequently will catch the calf first and use it to coax the mother to safety. This bond has historically been observed—and utilized— by people who came into contact with manatees. Friar Cristovao de Lisboa wrote in 1632 in *History of Animals and Trees of Maranhao*, "I saw a female get killed and skinned, and they threw the skin on the ground at the edge of the water. And the next day, going to get water, they found the offspring stretched out over the skin and they took it."

Manatee life centers around a few daily activities with no set schedule. Of course, much of the day is spent eating, while several more hours are spent resting, traveling, investigating curious objects, and socializing by "kissing," mouthing, bumping, or chasing other manatees. These activities occur intermittently throughout the day and night. During cold snaps in the winter, activities such as feeding may be regulated by daytime temperature cycles. Manatees also have

been known to schedule activities such as feeding and resting to avoid harassment by divers and boaters.

Manatees rest either suspended near the surface or lying on the bottom, usually for several hours at a time. On cold days when the water is warmer near the surface, manatees tend to rest at the surface. If resting on the bottom, they rise to the surface to breathe in an almost hypnotic state. Manatees generally surface to breathe every two to four minutes, but when bottom resting may not surface for twelve minutes.

Manatees frequently rub themselves against logs, rocks, ropes, and even the hulls of boats. Females tend to rub more than males, and often the areas they rub are places where glandular secretions may be produced, such as the genitals and around the eyes, armpits, and chin. Scratching may relieve itching, but some scientists speculate that it may also leave a scent message regarding the presence and reproductive condition of resident females.

Manatees within a group do not dominate others, nor are they territorial or aggressive. Groups form casually without regard to sex or age, with the exception of cow-calf pairs and temporary bachelor herds of juvenile males excluded from breeding. Occasionally, though, an individual manatee will instigate an activity that other manatees will follow. This may include games of "follow the leader," during which two or more manatees move together in

A Florida manatee stirs up bottom sediments while eating hydrilla.

ABOVE: *A Florida manatee rubs its head against a rock.*
RIGHT: *Male Florida manatees jostle for position around a female manatee in estrus.*

OPPOSITE PAGE:
TOP: *A female Florida manatee in estrus is pursued by six males in the Crystal River National Wildlife Refuge.*
BOTTOM: *Florida manatees frequently engage in tactile or sex play.*

single file, synchronizing their breathing, diving, change of direction, and other activities. Researcher John Reynolds watched five adult manatees in Blue Lagoon Lake body surf together for more than an hour in the flumes created by a salinity intrusion barrier. Four animals followed the lead of a fifth, calling to each other and nuzzling between rides. Manatees may play for hours, but generally only after they have fed and when they are not harassed.

Mating Behavior and Reproduction

The estrous cycle of mature female manatees lasts about a month. They can have more than one estrous cycle a year and usually continue cycling until they become pregnant. When a female manatee comes into estrus, she attracts a crowd of males, and together they form a mating herd that may stay together for between a week and a month. The bulls do not defend territories around the cow, but rather jostle each other in attempts to remain at her side. Each wishes to be the first to mate with her when she becomes receptive. As the bulls pursue the cow, she often swims into shoals or shallow water, twisting and turning violently, perhaps to prevent them from reaching her underside to mate. The fracas frequently attracts more males. Sometimes the female runs aground or slaps males with her tail, prompting unseasoned observers to call with reports of a manatee in distress. Once the female is receptive, she may mate with one to several males in quick succession. Mating can take place at the surface or underwater, and no single posture is assumed during copulation. Some pairs remain horizontal in the water column, others vertical. Frequently, the bull turns upside down and swims below the female, but mating can also take place with the animals on their sides, facing each other. After the female is impregnated, the mating herd breaks up and the males and female go their separate ways.

Most females first breed successfully when they are seven to nine years old. Some females may be physically able to breed as early as four or five years of age, but they may not be able to raise a calf successfully. Gestation generally lasts about a year, whereupon females find a quiet place to give birth alone. Calves can be born either head-first or tail-first. The cow usually produces one calf with each pregnancy, although twins are occasionally born. Other females may care for orphaned calves. A healthy female usually gives birth to a calf every three years or so, although a female that has lost her calf could have another within two years. Calves are born throughout the year, although in Florida more seem to be born in spring and summer.

Newborn manatee calves weigh an average of 66 pounds (30 kg) and range in length from 4 to 4.5 feet (1.2–1.4 m). A calf begins to nurse within a few hours of birth. Although it is born with teeth and will begin nibbling on plants within a few weeks, it continues to depend on milk for its nutrition. A manatee calf nurses underwater for up to three minutes from a single teat located in each of the mother's armpits. As it grows older, the calf will nurse longer and more often. Manatee milk contains more fats, proteins, and salt than does cow milk, but no lactose. Although a manatee calf is

Two Florida manatees rise to the surface for a breath.

A Florida manatee nurses her calf in a spring, Crystal River.

usually weaned by the time it is a year old, it stays with its mother for up to two years. Some calves spend their adolescent lives near their mothers as well.

The sex of a manatee is difficult to determine without viewing the underside of the animal. Both sexes have an umbilical scar midway along the belly; in males, the genital opening is located close to the umbilical scar, with the anus by itself near the tail. In females, both the anal and genital openings are close to the tail. A female can also be identified, of course, if it is accompanied by a nursing calf or if it is visibly rotund as a result of pregnancy.

Natural Mortality

Although Florida manatees have few natural predators, an average of 175 deaths occur each year. Some of these are due to natural causes, but many are caused directly by humans or indirectly by human activity. During 1997, a total of 242 manatee deaths were recorded in Florida. This number is below the record 415 deaths documented in 1996 (which included a major red tide-related die-off), but well above both the ten-year (1986-1995) annual average of 161 and the five-year (1991-1995) average of 175. In fact, it is the second-highest total since scientists began keeping records in 1974.

The largest identifiable mortality factors are collisions with boats and barges. These and other human-related causes of death are discussed in detail in chapter 5. Most natural manatee deaths are perinatal or related to catastrophic events, including unusually cold weather and infrequent, but lethal, outbreaks of red tide. Other natural causes of death include disease, parasitism, injuries unrelated to human activity.

Perinatal deaths are those that occur around the time of birth, from the later stages of gestation to the first few months of life. The deaths of newborn manatees, stillborns, and miscarried fetuses are grouped in this category. A baby manatee may die from poor nutrition, infection, diarrhea, or separation from its mother. Perinatal deaths are most common from March through July—probably because that is when the bulk of calving occurs—and account for about 25 percent of all manatee deaths.

Although a manatee calf is born with teeth and begins nibbling on plants within a few weeks of birth, it continues to depend on its mother's milk for nutrition for nearly a year.

From 1974 to 1992, 425 perinatal deaths were recorded, an average of 24 deaths a year. In 1997, 61 perinatal deaths were tallied.

As discussed earlier in this chapter, cold weather can be fatal to manatees. Following a severe cold spell in the winter of 1989–90, 56 manatee carcasses whose deaths were attributed to cold stress were recovered in five southeastern states. Because cold-related mortality was not listed as a separate category until 1986, exact numbers of cold-related deaths before that time are unknown. However, exposure to cold is believed to have caused many deaths in the winters of 1977, 1981, and 1984.

In March 1996, more than 150 manatees died along the southwest Florida Gulf Coast (10 percent of the Gulf Coast population) after an outbreak of red tide. Red tide is caused by a bloom of algae—dinoflagellates of the genus *Gymnodinium* (and possibly other genera as well)—that stains seawater reddish-brown. These blooms occur naturally in the world's oceans and are common along the Gulf Coast. Unfortunately, one byproduct of red tide is brevetoxin, a powerful irritant that attacks a part of the nervous system that controls breathing. Many manatees literally suffocated after exposure to brevetoxin, said Dr. Scott Wright, chief manatee pathologist for the State of Florida. Necropsies of the affected manatees revealed discolored, fluid-filled lungs.

The 1996 red tide was not the first to kill manatees. In spring 1982, 37 manatee deaths in southwest Florida were blamed on exposure to red-tide neurotoxins in the Fort Myers area (Caloosahatchee River basin). Then, biologists had no sooner finished assessing the impact of the death toll from 1996 when another red tide occurred in November 1997. This outbreak, fortunately, was less severe, but another 16 manatees perished from brevetoxin poisoning. While red tides are a natural event, some scientists speculate that the increasing frequency and severity of red tides may be linked to higher levels of pollutants in the world's oceans.

Antillean Manatee

The Antillean manatee (*Trichechus manatus manatus*) is virtually indistinguishable from the Florida manatee by appearance alone. An average adult Antillean manatee weighs about 1,200 pounds (500 kg) and measures about 10 feet (3 m). Large adult females may weigh more than 2,200 pounds (1,000 kg) and reach a maximum length of about 10 feet (3 m). Like the Florida manatee, Antillean manatees live in coastal areas, seeking sheltered bays, estuaries, and slow-moving rivers with plenty of aquatic vegetation on which to feed. They also can move freely between salt and fresh water. Scientists believe most aspects of their social and reproductive behavior and use of habitat are similar as well.

The Antillean manatee ranges throughout the greater Caribbean area (including Mexico and southern Texas) and northeastern South America, including Brazil, Surinam, Guyana, Trinidad, Venezuela, Colombia, Panama, Costa Rica, Nicaragua, Honduras, Guatemala, and Belize. More than sixty manatees are thought to live along the coast of Puerto Rico, and perhaps thirty-two live along the coast of Haiti. According to records from the sixteenth and seventeenth centuries, the Antillean manatee was once found almost as far south as Rio de Janeiro, Brazil. Many of the regions in the Antillean manatee's range have not been completely surveyed, so neither the complete distribution of the species nor a good estimate of its population is known.

The Antillean manatee is not evenly distributed throughout its range, in large part because of the patchiness of suitable habitat. Manatees need both vegetation and fresh water, and local populations in some areas appear to move in conjunction with the rainy season. Manatees move upriver when water levels are high and retreat downstream when water levels drop in the dry season. Antillean manatees are relatively abundant in Mexico and Belize where large areas of quality habitat still exist.

Range of the Antillean manatee

An Antillean manatee feeds on Thallasia *seagrass.*

Amazonian manatees swim under the floating aquatic plants common in their range. Photograph © Nick Gordon

Antillean manatees are susceptible to many of the same causes of death as Florida manatees, although they rarely encounter water cold enough to cause difficulties. Entanglement in fishing nets and collisions with motorboats are leading causes of death, and although Antillean manatees are protected in nearly every country they inhabit, they are still often hunted for meat, either for personal consumption or for sale on the black market.

Amazonian Manatee

Many scientists consider the Amazonian manatee (*Trichechus inunguis*), known among local people throughout its range as *peixe-boi* (Portuguese for oxfish) or *vaca marina* (Spanish for sea cow), as the most specialized of the living species of manatees. It was not recognized as a distinct species until 1830, and then it was virtually forgotten except by those who hunted it.

Range

The Amazonian manatee is the smallest living sirenian and the only one restricted to fresh water. Endemic to the Amazon basin, it prefers water temperatures ranging from 77° to 86° F (25°–30° C) and seeks calm flood plain lakes and the channels of whitewater rivers with abundant vegetation. (*Whitewater* here refers to water that is less acidic and high in suspended sediments and nutrients, not fast-moving like "whitewater" rivers in North America.) This region has a marked dry season and wet season, and water levels may change as much as 30 to 50 feet (10–15 m) between seasons.

The Amazonian manatee's range includes the Amazon River and its tributaries in Brazil, along the Brazil-Guyana border, in Peru, in Colombia, and in Ecuador. According to sirenian researcher Daryl Domning, both Amazonian and Antillean manatees frequent regions near the broad mouth of the Amazon River in Brazil. This is likely the only place in the world where two species of sirenian occur together.

Physical Description

Smaller and slimmer than its West Indian and West African cousins, the Amazonian manatee may measure up to 9.2 feet (2.8 m) in length and weigh as much as 1,056 pounds (480 kg). By comparison, the average West Indian manatee measures 10 feet (three meters) long and weighs about 1,200 pounds

(500 kg). Its color varies from dark gray to black, and most animals have distinctive white or pink unpigmented patches on the belly. There is no difference in size between males and females.

The Amazonian manatee is different from West Indian and West African manatees in other ways as well. Its specific name, *inunguis*, means "without nails" and refers to the lack of toenails on its pectoral flippers; both West Indian and West African manatees have toenails. Amazonian manatees also have proportionally longer flippers, smaller teeth, and a longer, narrower rostrum (the anterior portion of the skull) than other manatee species. The skin of the Amazonian manatee after infancy is smooth, unlike the pebbled texture of the skin of other manatees. On the cellular level, Amazonian manatees have fifty-six chromosomes, while the West Indian manatee has forty-eight. The scientific community once believed this chromosomal difference left little chance of hybridization between Amazonian and West Indian (Antillean) manatees where the two species share habitat at the mouth of the Amazon, but new unpublished findings indicate hybridization may indeed occur. The number of chromosomes in the West African manatee

Amazon River

Pacific Ocean

SOUTH AMERICA

Atlantic Ocean

● Range of the Amazonian manatee

has not been determined.

The Amazonian manatee, like other manatees, has only molars. Vestigial incisors remain in the upper jaw, but they never become functional. As with other manatees, the molars of Amazonian manatees are stimulated by chewing to move horizontally from the back of the jaw forward. These molars replace those that have become worn and fallen out at the front, prompting some scientists to dub them "conveyor belt teeth." The entire tooth row moves forward about one millimeter a month throughout a manatee's life.

As mentioned before, the rostrum of the Amazonian manatee is narrower than in other species. It is also deflected about 30°. Thus the Amazonian manatee's "forehead" curves downward less than that of the West Indian manatee, whose rostrum is deflected about 38°. This lesser curvature of the head, together with specific features of the muscles and articulation of the neck, appears to be an adaptation for feeding on floating and emergent aquatic plants. In other physiological aspects, including its bones, digestive system, and lungs, it is similar to its West Indian and West African cousins. Like other manatees, it can stay submerged for up to twenty minutes when resting.

Metabolic Rate and Temperature Regulation

Like other manatees, the Amazonian manatee has a low metabolic rate (about 36 percent of what is typical for a mammal its size) and an intolerance of cold water. Scientists believe the low metabolic rate is a result of evolving in a stable, warm-water environment, and that it allows a manatee to hold its breath for long periods when submerged. The Amazonian manatees' low metabolism may also allow it to survive long periods without food.

Social Behavior

Unlike the Florida manatee, which frequently approaches boats and cavorts with swimmers, the Amazonian manatee is elusive and practically impossible to observe in the wild. When it rises silently every few minutes to breathe, it never exposes more than the tip of its snout. Its secretive nature is probably in large part a response to centuries of hunting by humans. Also, the water where it lives is usually murky, which prevents observation of the animals underwater.

Within the last century, large herds of feeding Amazonian manatees were reported. Now, when they can be found at all, they are seen feeding in small, loosely organized groups of four to eight individuals.

Most of what is known about Amazonian manatees is based on the results of studies conducted by members of the Brazilian Manatee Project, or Projeto Peixe-Boi, initiated in 1975 by the Brazilian government's Instituto Nacional de Pesquisas da Amazonia (INPA) at Manaus, in the heart of the Brazilian Amazon. While research regarding distribution and basic ecology was done with wild populations of manatees, studies on various aspects of physiology, behavior, and captive rearing of young and adult animals involved manatees housed at the Aquatic Mammal Laboratory of INPA. Most manatees arrived at INPA as orphaned calves and were hand-raised and bottle-fed until weaned. Rescued individuals that could not be released remained in captivity for study, eliminating the need to capture more wild manatees.

Studies of these captive animals indicate that their social and reproductive behavior resembles that of Florida manatees. Captive manatees often clasp each other with pectoral flippers and chase each other in the water, engage in sex play, and communicate with high-pitched squeals. The only lasting bonds form between a female manatee and her calf. Based on studies done by Dr. Robin Best at INPA, captive Amazonian manatees spent four hours each day resting, eight hours feeding, and twelve hours simply swimming. A radio-tagged manatee that was followed for twenty days was equally active during the day and night and traveled about 1.7 miles (2.7 km) a day.

Like Florida manatees, Amazonian manatees form mating herds when a female comes into estrus and attracts a crowd of bulls. Wild Amazonian manatees gather together in feeding areas, but—contrary to observations of captive manatees—little interaction between animals has been observed. In at least one instance, captive manatees were observed assisting another that was in trouble. One of the manatees was having trouble reaching the surface to breathe, prompting two of its poolmates to support it on either side and help the weakened manatee rise to the surface.

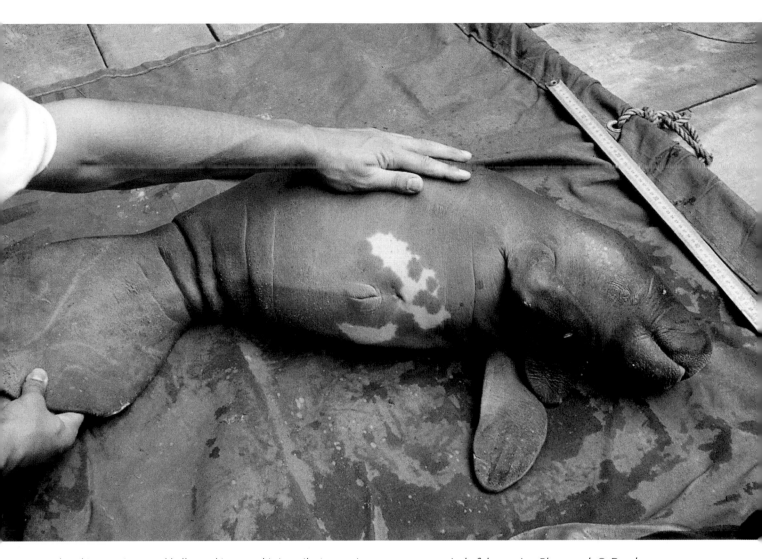

The white, unpigmented belly markings on this juvenile Amazonian manatee are typical of the species. Photograph © Daryl Domning

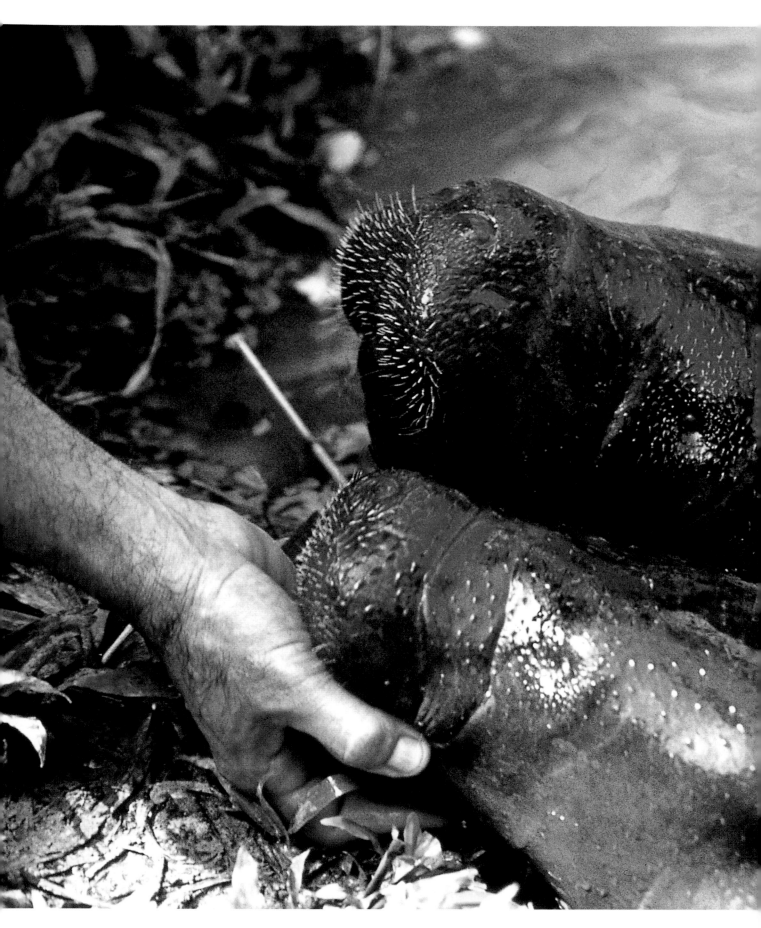

Two Amazonian manatees sidle up to
the shore to have their heads scratched
by a member of the Brazilian Manatee
Project. Photograph © Fernando
Trujillo/Innerspace Visions

Reproduction

Reproduction in Amazonian manatees is closely linked with the hydrologic cycle of the Amazon Basin. Research done by Robin Best has shown that most copulation occurs when the waters of the Amazon begin rising from December through June, with most births coming between February and May. Best believed that during this period, the plants on which manatees feed are abundant and nutritious, allowing females to replace the energy they've lost during the last stage of pregnancy and the beginning of lactation. Amazonian manatees probably become sexually mature between five and ten years old (based on estimates made for the Florida manatee). Each successful pregnancy produces one calf, and a female may become pregnant every two-and-a-half to five years. Newborns are at least 30 inches (80 cm) long, and captive animals increase in length by about one-half inch (1.4 cm) per week. There is no information about the weight of Amazonian manatees at birth, but captive animals gained an average of about two pounds (one kg) per week. Captive calves were weaned at about a year old.

Movement and Habitat Use

While Amazonian manatees do not migrate to escape cold weather, they do migrate in response to seasonal changes in water levels and the availability of food. As water levels rise during the rainy season (December to June), vast, flooded, nutrient-rich areas called *várzea* form along the rivers (primarily whitewater rivers), producing enormous quantities of aquatic and semi-aquatic plants, many of which are favored by manatees. Manatees also travel into the igapó, or flooded forest, to feed on tender, new plant growth. As the river levels fall from July through November during the dry season, manatees move into river channels, deep-water canals, or permanent—usually blackwater—lakes. These lakes are much less acidic than the blackwater swamps and rivers of the southern United States. If a dry season is exceptionally long, manatees may die of starvation. Because Amazonian manatees migrate in response to changing water levels, movement patterns of manatees in the upper and middle Amazon basin may be completely different from those of manatees in other areas.

Mortality

Amazonian manatees face dangers from natural predators that other manatees do not. Jaguars, caimans (a relative of the alligator), and sharks have all been known to prey on Amazonian manatees. Human predation is a problem as well, despite legal protection, particularly during the dry season, when manatees are forced to congregate in small areas of suitable habitat, leaving them susceptible to poaching.

While no precise figures exist for the number of Amazonian manatees remaining in the wild, they are considered rare or close to extinction in Peru and Colombia and uncommon throughout their range in eastern Ecuador. Hunting deserves most of the blame, although catastrophic natural events also have contributed, such as the long dry season of 1963, during which hundreds of manatees died when lakes and rivers dried up.

West African Manatee

The West African manatee (*Trichechus senegalensis*) is thought by paleontologists to have originated from West Indian manatees that crossed the Atlantic less than five million years ago. Because environmental conditions on both sides of the Atlantic were similar then and continue to be similar now, there has been no evolutionary pressure for the species to develop remarkably different characteristics. For this reason, the two species are remarkably similar in appearance, physiology, reproductive and social behavior, and habitat requirements.

Whereas the West Indian manatee is perhaps the most studied sirenian in the world, the West African manatee is the least known, in part because there is no center of research for this species as there are for other manatees and the dugong. West African manatees are widely distributed in fresh water and coastal marine waters in a dozen countries from Senegal to Angola in western Central Africa. In Liberia and in other west African countries, the manatee is called "mammy-water." In Gabon, the manatee is called *manga*. The historical range of West African manatees seems to differ little from their current overall range, although their numbers have dwindled and local populations have been exterminated by hunting and habitat loss. They have few predators other than humans and the occasional crocodile or shark.

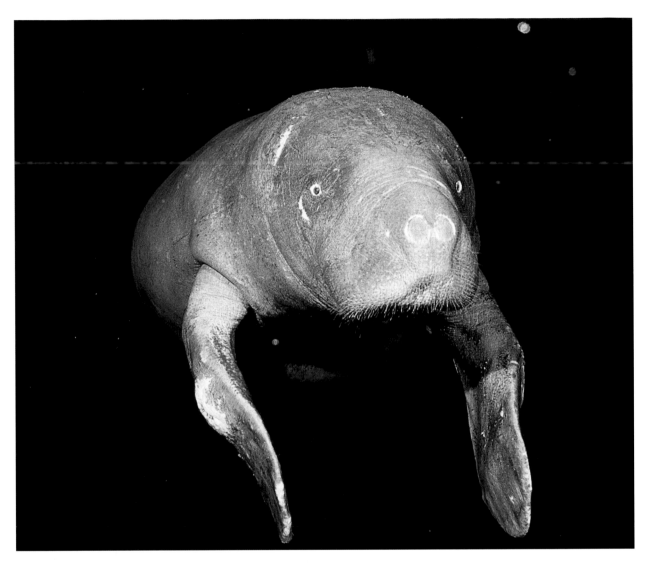

A West African manatee swims in its tank at the Toba Aquarium, Toba, Japan. The West African manatee is the least-studied living sirenian species, and photographs of them in the wild are rare. Photograph © Toba Aquarium

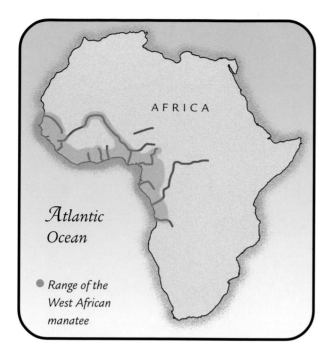

Atlantic Ocean

AFRICA

● *Range of the West African manatee*

because of its blunt snout.

Diet and Feeding

West African manatees rely heavily on a variety of floating aquatic plants, as well as on some submerged plants. When these plants are not available, manatees may graze mangrove leaves or shoreline vegetation. In some areas, mangrove leaves provide the bulk of the manatee diet, and if mangroves die off, as they did along the Allahein River in coastal Gambia, the manatee population can decline dramatically. Like the West Indian manatee in Puerto Rico, West African manatees have been reported to feed opportunistically on clams.

Movement and Habitat

West African manatees use coastal rivers in much the same way as Antillean and Amazonian manatees. They move far upstream during the wet season to feed on the lush new vegetation in flooded areas, then drift downstream toward the coast as river levels fall during the dry season. Occasionally, manatees linger longer than they should in tributaries and lakes connected to larger rivers and become trapped by falling water levels.

West African manatees are protected in Senegal, Guinea, Sierra Leone, Liberia, Ivory Coast, Ghana, Togo, Dahomey, Nigeria, Gabon, Cameroon, Congo, Zaire, and Angola. Hunting by native people and incidental capture in gill nets remains a problem. Manatee meat is openly consumed and even sold in markets in some African countries, including Sierra Leone. Furthermore, proposed hydroelectric dams threaten manatees and their habitat on major rivers in countries such as Nigeria and Gambia. Because manatees are highly valued as a traditional food source, and because many African nations are placing great hope in hydroelectric power, biologists worry that conserving the West African manatee and its habitat may prove extremely difficult.

Like West Indian manatees, West African manatees prefer quiet coastal areas, large rivers, lagoons, and connected lakes where they have easy access to fresh water and adequate food. They also need water that is at least 64° F (18° C).

Physical Description

The West African and West Indian manatees are comparable in size and shape, have the same brown to gray wrinkled skin, and have similar sparse coverings of body hair. There are, however, a few notable differences between the two species. The skull bones of the West African manatee are different, and its body is not quite as rotund as that of its West Indian relative. Its rostrum is deflected downward less than the West Indian manatee's. Scientists believe that this adaptive characteristic reflects the West African manatee's primary diet of floating aquatic plants rather than bottom vegetation. Its eyes bulge more than those of the West Indian manatee, and it has been described as pug-nosed

A manatee calf nurses from one of its mother's teats, located at the base of the flipper.

CHAPTER 3

The Dugong
and Steller's sea cow

L E F T :   *The dugong has the widest distribution*
of any of the sirenians, living in tropical and subtropical coastal and
island waters of the western Pacific and Indian oceans.
A B O V E :   *A dugong swims over a shallow-water coral reef.*

ANCIENT MEMBERS OF the family Dugongidae are among the most common sirenians in the fossil record. One species, the dugong (*Dugong dugon*), survives today. The Steller's sea cow (*Hydrodamalis gigas*), a related species that lived in the North Pacific Ocean until only couple of hundred years ago, is believed to have descended from *Metaxytherium*, a widespread genus of dugongids that lived during the Miocene (5 million to 25 million years ago) and Pliocene (two to five million years ago). Sadly, the Steller's sea cow was hunted to extinction around 1768 by fur traders twenty-seven years after Georg Steller brought it to the attention of the scientific community.

The Dugong

Most Americans could probably identify a photo of a manatee and maybe tell you that the manatee is an endangered species. They may have heard about manatees on a news report, licked a manatee stamp from the U.S. Postal Service's Endangered Species series, or seen one on a marine life calendar. Ask an American about a dugong, however, and the response is invariably a blank stare, followed by

"What's a dugong?" This reaction is to be expected, considering there are no dugongs—in captivity or in the wild—within several thousand miles of the Americas or Europe. This distribution has been the case for most of recorded history. And when European explorers came across dugongs or their remains, they were often mistaken for something else—manatees, hippos, and, yes, mermaids.

The association with mermaids, of course, dates back to sailors from classical times who had been too long at sea—in the sun—and without the company of women. You only need to look at a picture of a dugong to see the imagination needed to turn a large, bewhiskered marine mammal into an alluring, naked woman-fish. The popular depiction of a mermaid more closely resembles the dugong than the manatee, because a mermaid possesses the forked, dolphin-like flukes and less rotund build of the dugong.

Confusing a dugong with a hippo or manatee is somewhat easier to understand. In 1688, William Dampier, an English explorer sailing in the Indian Ocean along the western coast of Australia, noted that "manatees" were common there. He had seen

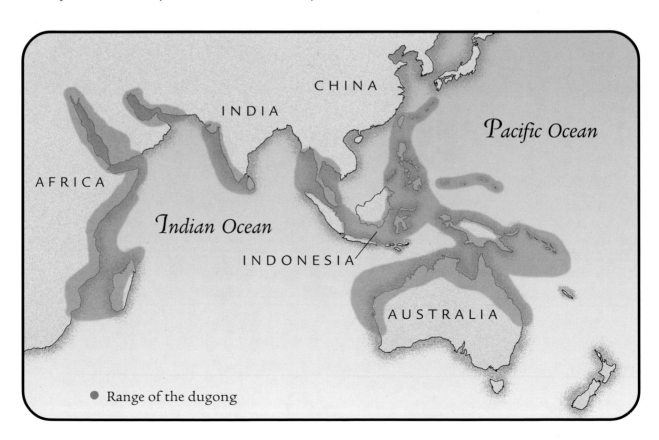

● Range of the dugong

OPPOSITE PAGE: *An adult dugong swims in the waters of coastal Australia.*

manatees during cruises to the Americas and assumed, without getting a close look, that the dugongs were the same. On a later voyage in 1699,
Dampier found the "head and boans of a Hippopotamus" with teeth up to 8 inches (20 cm) long in
the stomach of a shark caught in Shark Bay, also
along Australia's west coast. That shark would have
had to swim a very long distance at great speed to
reach Australian waters with African hippo bones
still in its gut (even if a hippo had succumbed to
the unlikely urge to head for the beach and swim in
the surf). Dampier's "hippopotamus" remains are
believed by modern biologists to have actually been
the skull and tusks of a dugong.

Traditional names for the dugong throughout
their Indo-Pacific range reinforce the popular perception that dugongs are something other than
what they truly are—graceful, entirely aquatic, primarily herbivorous, marine mammals. The Mala-
gasy name for the dugong, according to a letter

*A dugong browses on seagrass (Amphibolis antartica) in
its winter feeding grounds in Shark Bay, Australia.*

printed in *Sirenews*, a newsletter for Sirenia scientists, is *lambondana*, which means "wild pig of the
coral." The dugong is known in many Asian countries as "sea pig" and is often referred to in East African countries as a type of hippo. And of course, it
is frequently hailed—like the manatee—as "sea cow."

The English word *dugong* comes from *duyong*
in Malay. The dugong is also known as *mudu oora* in
Sinhalese and *avolia* and *kadalpanni* in Tamil. It
has the widest distribution of any of the sirenians,
living in tropical and subtropical coastal and island
waters of the western Pacific and Indian oceans
from East Africa to the Solomon Islands and Vanu-
atu, including the Red Sea, the Persian Gulf, Asia,
Micronesia, Melanesia, and Australia. Its range extends from about 26°–27° north and south of the
equator, spanning the waters of more than forty
countries. Most of the world's dugongs live in the
waters of northern Australia, where they are a protected species. Dugong populations are widely scattered and declining throughout most of the rest of
their range. Australian researcher Dr. Helene Marsh,
a world authority on dugongs, estimates that 8,100
dugongs may live in the western half of northern
Australia's Gulf of Carpentaria. More than 45,000
dugongs are thought to roam the Torres Strait between New Guinea and Australia, and as many as
70,000 may be roaming Australian territorial waters. No one is sure how many dugongs exist elsewhere.

Dugongs are often found in the shallow water—less than 16.5 feet (5 m) deep—of bays, shallows, and shoals that support extensive beds of
seagrass protected from rough seas and high winds.
They have been spotted, however, in water as deep
as 122 feet (37 m) and near reefs up to 48 miles (80
km) offshore. They occasionally move into river
mouths and up creeks.

Biologists in Australia, where most dugong
research takes place, are adamant in pointing out
that dugongs are not tropical Indo-Pacific manatees and go to great lengths to relate the differences
between the animals. To wit:

Dr. Paul Anderson writes, "Mention of the
manatee brings me to a sensitive point. The dugong is not just the manatee of the eastern tropical
oceans. Dugongs and manatees are, zoologically
speaking, about as alike as camels and giraffes. Just
as the latter are in separate zoological Families belonging to the same Order, so [are] dugongs and

When cruising, a dugongs tucks its pectoral flippers against its sides.

ABOVE: *A dugong, surfacing to breathe in a nearly horizontal position, moves slowly forward.*
RIGHT: *A skeleton of a male dugong displayed at the Western Australian Museum.*

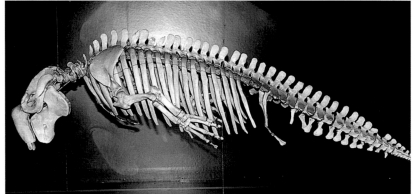

manatees. . . . Manatees are predominantly animals of quiet fresh or estuarine waters where they propel their tubby bodies with ponderous but not ungraceful undulations of broad, rug-like tails. Dugongs, swift, streamlined and with whale-like flukes, are marine."

Other disparities exist as well. First, dugongs grow short tusks, unlike manatees, and dugongs' teeth are much less specialized than manatees. Minor physiological and anatomical differences include the shape and possibly the capabilities of the kidneys. Dugongs often rest and feed in much deeper water, farther offshore than manatees, and feed in a somewhat different manner. Some data suggest they cannot stay submerged for nearly as long as manatees. In some areas, they gather to graze in large herds, returning to forage in the same area for up to a month, an adaptive behavior that helps propagate the species of seagrasses they prefer. Manatees, on the other hand, generally congregate only during cold weather or during mating and do not graze single areas so intensively. Dugongs take much longer to become sexually mature than manatees. Finally, competition among male dugongs for mating rights is usually more violent than among male manatees.

Physical Description
A dugong has a torpedo-shaped body that begins with a blunt, remotely pig-like head, broadens near the pectoral fins, and then tapers before ending with the wide, split flukes of the tail. Unlike the manatee, it has no fingernails on the pectoral fins. The dugong's thick skin is gray to gray-brown and smooth, with a sparse covering of short hairs. The skin is about 1.4 inches (3.5 cm) thick, including its thin layer of fat. An adult dugong averages about 9 feet (2.7 m) in length and weighs 550 to 660 pounds (250–300 kg). A large adult may measure up to 11 feet (3.3 m) and weigh more than 880 pounds (400 kg).

A pair of valve-like nostrils is located at the tip of a dugong's snout, so it needs only expose a small portion of its head above the water's surface to breathe. Its muzzle is turned distinctly downward, an adaptive reflection of its bottom-feeding habits, and ends with a broad, flattened area called the rostral disk. Its enormous, horseshoe-shaped upper lip is covered with bristles that it uses to locate and manipulate seagrass into its mouth. Small, delicate

species of seagrass are dug up by the roots with a fleshy knob at the front of the upper jaw, which is bounded on either side by a pair of short tusks that appear in mature males and some old females.

A dugong's eyes are small and its ears are pinholes in the side of its head, but both its sight and hearing are considered good. Scientists currently believe that dugongs produce only a few sounds—including chirps, squeaks, and barks—which they presumably produce with the larynx. Vision and hearing help dugong cows and calves to establish and maintain their strong social bond.

A dugong moves by undulating its flukes, and when cruising tucks the pectoral flippers against its sides. It uses its flippers for braking and turning, as well as to keep its nostrils above the waves when surfacing in rough seas. When a dugong is idle or resting, it lets its flippers droop. When feeding, a dugong may use them to prop itself off the bottom, but dugong flippers are probably less flexible than those of manatees and do not seem to be used for grasping food. Dugongs are generally slow swimmers, cruising at about two to four miles per hour (3.2–6.4 km), but they can accelerate to more than fifteen miles per hour (25 km) for short distances.

Dugong Anatomy and Physiology
The dugong's skeleton is similar to a manatee's, with thick, heavy bones, no hind limbs, and vestigial pelvic bones remaining in its musculature. It has seven cervical vertebrae as opposed to six in a manatee. Dr. Daryl Domning recently discovered that the pelvic bones of male and female dugongs are shaped differently, allowing the sex of a dugong to be determined from skeletal remains. As with manatees, the sex of a live dugong is determined by the position of the anal and genital openings in relation to the umbilical scar, as well as by the presence of teats under the armpits of female dugongs.

Unlike the highly evolved, conveyor-belt molars of manatees, dugong molars are simple and peglike, best suited for tearing small, soft, low-fiber, highly nutritious seagrasses. These make up the bulk of the dugong's diet. Although dugongs do not replace their teeth, they overcome tooth wear with the continuous growth of the last two molars in each quadrant of the jaw. A male dugong's distinctive tusks erupt through the gums from the upper jaw at puberty, when they are about nine or ten years old. Females have tusks imbedded in their upper jaw as well, but these rarely erupt to grow like those of males. Scientists can count the growth layers in the tusks to determine a dugong's age, much like the growth layers in the inner ear bones of manatees or the rings of a tree. Analyses of tusks tell us that dugongs may live to more than seventy years, a life span similar to that of humans.

The lungs, digestive system, brain, and most other physiological features of the dugong resemble those of manatees. The kidneys, however, are quite different. Unlike manatees, dugongs are able to survive in a predominantly saltwater environment. Scientists think the dugong's kidneys may produce urine that is concentrated enough to remove the salt taken in with food. They are unsure, however, whether this capacity alone allows dugongs to exist in saltwater.

Diving and Surfacing

Dugongs generally surface to breathe at shorter intervals than manatees. When dugongs are grazing, they surface every minute or so, spending one or two seconds at the surface before submerging again. Cows with calves surface less frequently than unaccompanied adults, as do adults that are investigating a boat or other unfamiliar object. Dugongs rarely stay down for more than three minutes.

When a dugong surfaces, it does so at a nearly horizontal position, moving slowly forward. It exhales just below or at the surface and then inhales before submerging once again. In calm water, surfacing dugongs are often overlooked because only the nostrils are exposed, and these break the surface for little more than a second. If seas are rough, the dugong will rise at a steeper angle, throwing its head back to clear the waves as it inhales. A dugong feeding in calm, shallow water may only breathe once before submerging to graze. A dugong feeding in rough seas will breathe up to five times, resting just below the surface between breaths, before diving to forage again.

According to Paul Anderson, a dugong arches its back and rolls forward, raising the middle of its back above the surface, when beginning a foraging dive. A traveling or idle dugong surfaces to breathe while moving forward, but doesn't arch its back or roll. A dugong that surfaces vertically to investigate an object above the surface submerges by sinking tail first.

Studies have shown that dugongs, like manatees, are not suited to prolonged exertion and cannot stay submerged for very long. The ability of sirenians to carry oxygen in the blood and muscles is poor compared to pinnipeds and cetaceans. A dugong that is chased or forced to flee at top speed (from a speed boat, for example) tires quickly and must begin surfacing more frequently within two or three minutes.

Metabolism and Susceptibility to Cold

Dugongs are believed to have a low metabolic rate similar to that of manatees. However, little information is available regarding the effect of cold on dugongs. They seem to be sensitive to cooler water temperatures that occur during the winter at the southern extremes of their range in Australia. They either migrate seasonally to areas with warmer water or move locally to deeper water where the temperature is more stable.

In Shark Bay, for example, the winter distribution of dugongs is thought to be tied to water temperature. Dr. Helene Marsh and her team conducted aerial surveys over Shark Bay and found fewer than 4 percent of dugongs sighted to be in surface water colder than 64° F (18° C). In eastern Moreton Bay on the east coast of Australia, dugongs were spotted feeding heavily over sandbanks in winter surface waters of 63° to 64° F (17°–18° C), but these animals regularly traveled more than seven miles (12 km) between their feeding areas and warm ocean waters outside the bay, a journey they did not make during the summer when bay waters were warmer. More than 60 percent of dugongs seen in Shark Bay in July 1989 (winter in Australia) were in water thirty-three to sixty-six feet (10–20 m) deep, where the temperature remains somewhat more stable and warm.

Diet and Feeding

Dugongs are generally restricted to coastal areas because they depend on seagrasses for food. They prefer to forage on seagrass beds along the edges of offshore shoals or around points, where they have easy access to both shallow and deep water. Dugongs avoid confined bays or narrow inlets, even when the water is more sheltered and seagrass more abundant.

The leaves, stems, and rhizomes of several species of seagrasses provide food for dugongs, which are strictly bottom-feeders. Feeding dugongs often

A dugong opens its mouth to reveal its tusks, a possibly aggressive display.

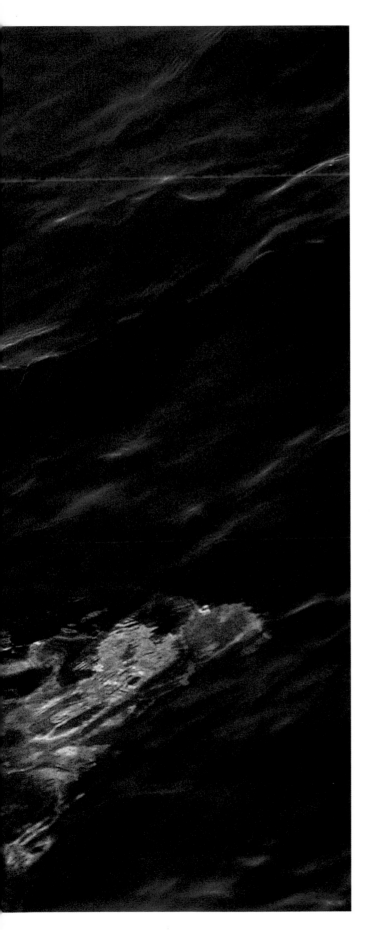

leave visible, serpentine paths in seagrass beds called "feeding trails," where the plants have been grazed to bare sand. Because of their simple, peglike teeth, dugongs target seagrasses that are tender, will break easily, and are low in fiber. Dugongs only eat algae when seagrass is not available. They will even avoid seagrass with heavy growths of algae on the leaves.

Dugongs frequently feed in much deeper water than manatees. Large groups of dugongs have been spotted in water more than thirty-three feet (10 m) deep, and feeding trails have been seen in water more than seventy-six feet (28 m) deep. Results from aerial surveys suggest that deep-water seagrass meadows are found at most of the major dugong areas in Australia, including the Starcke River region, Shark Bay, Princess Charlotte Bay, Torres Strait, and Hervey Bay. Tidal ranges and currents, water turbidity, and wind intensity and direction all influence where and when dugongs feed. Although most dugongs forage over the entire 24-hour day, disturbance from heavy boating activity and/or hunting may force some populations to feed primarily at night.

How dugongs forage depends on what they are eating. When grazing low-growing seagrasses in soft-bottom sediments, dugongs root into the bottom to extract entire plants, including rhizomes, stems, and leaves, raising clouds of sediment in the process. Dugongs eating tall seagrasses in hard sediments—in which case the rhizomes are not accessible—strip the leaves, but rarely eat the whole plant. According to Paul Anderson, when dugongs feed heavily in an area and remove much of the seagrass, they reduce the cover for small fish and invertebrates and leave the area vulnerable to further damage by wave action. Thus, feeding dugongs maintain a seagrass community at an immature, fast-growing stage, which may cause a decline in the many fish and shrimp that depend on tall, mature seagrass beds for cover and food. This impact may bring efforts to conserve dugongs into conflict with efforts to protect and manage seagrass beds for other purposes, such as fishing.

How Dugong Grazing Impacts Seagrass Beds
Research conducted by Tony Preen in Moreton Bay

A dugong surfaces to breathe in Shark Bay, Australia.

A dugong stirs bottom sediments while feeding on seagrass.

has shown that dugongs prefer to feed in seagrass communities dominated by early pioneer species. A pioneer species is one that successfully establishes itself in a previously barren environment, thus starting an ecological cycle of life. Pioneer species, such as *Halophila ovalis* and *Halophila uninervis*, are typically more tender and nutritious and less fibrous than other species. Dugongs will also selectively feed on patches of these species within other communities. When dugongs feed in mixed seagrass communities, they concentrate on their favorite species. Because of their wide muzzles, however, they cannot isolate individual plants, and so often consume less desirable vegetation as well.

Dugongs in Moreton Bay usually feed in large herds of more than 100 animals and will graze the same location for a month or more. Heavy grazing significantly impacts the seagrass community, reducing the density of seagrass shoots, including the underground rhizomes, by as much as 95 percent. Despite the intensity and impact of dugong grazing, a seagrass community usually recovers within a few months, often to the benefit of pioneer species—which thrive in recently disturbed areas—over other species.

Seagrass' quick recovery depends in part on the plants' growth characteristics, and in part on the way dugongs feed. Dugongs do not graze like cattle, with each animal cropping adjoining small areas. Instead, each dugong forages in a long, meandering swath about as wide as its muzzle. Individual feeding trails overlap and intersect under heavy

grazing, but small tufts of seagrass are always missed. From these tufts, new seagrass spreads. This type of impact differs from disturbances caused by sedimentation, ice scour, or other forms of seagrass die-off. In these situations, the effect is more uniform, and individual tufts rarely survive. Seagrass can then recover only through colonization by seeds or propagules, or by the spread of neighboring communities that were not affected. This type of recovery, too, can occur quickly.

By grazing intensively in large herds, dugongs increase the nutritional value of favorite feeding grounds. Tony Preen writes, "seagrass responds to cropping or clipping of leaves by increasing nitrogen levels and decreasing levels of lignin or ash in new growth." Thus new seagrass shoots are more nutritious to dugongs than older growth. Repeated, heavy grazing ensures that large areas of seagrass will remain in an "immature, rapidly growing state," providing the dugongs with gardens of favored seagrasses at their most nutritious stages. In mixed seagrass communities, heavy grazing increases the ratio of favored pioneer species to other seagrasses.

Omnivory in Dugongs

Moreton Bay lies in the eastern Australian subtropics. Seagrass in the bay, as in other subtropical areas, follows a seasonal pattern of abundance and productivity. In summer and fall, the growing season, seagrass is usually plentiful. New shoots provide nutritious food for dugongs and other grazers. In winter and early spring, seagrasses put out little new growth. The older leaves are more fibrous and less nutritious, with lower levels of nitrogen and soluble carbohydrate. Tony Preen has noted that in Moreton Bay, when their preferred seagrasses are nutritionally poor, dugongs deliberately feed on small invertebrates called ascidians. He thinks these animals may supplement the dugongs' intake of protein. In tropical areas, dugongs are not omnivorous, probably because seagrass growth differs by season. Also, Preen suggests, ascidians in tropical areas may possess a chemical defense that makes them distasteful.

Loss of Seagrass and Its Impact on Dugongs

A large-scale loss of seagrass can doom dugongs. Such an event happened in 1992, after two floods and a cyclone killed more than 400 square miles (1,000 km²) of seagrass in Hervey Bay in eastern

A dugong stirs a cloud of bottom sediments in an attempt to escape from pesky pilot fish, which follow the marine mammals in search of food scraps.

Australia. An aerial survey in August 1988 counted more than 1,750 dugongs over southern Hervey Bay. By November 1992, eight months after the floods and cyclone, only seventy-one dugongs remained. As many as 1,000 dugongs are believed to have fled the region, many to the neighboring Great Sandy Strait. Nearly 100 carcasses were recovered, some more than 540 miles (900 km) south of Hervey Bay. Most of the dugongs apparently died of starvation, six to eight months after the loss of seagrass. They probably tried to survive on algae, dead seagrass rhizomes, and anoxic (oxygen-poor) sediment.

Dugongs are returning to Hervey Bay as the seagrass beds recover. A survey in December 1993 estimated 600 dugongs in the region. Due in part to the slow reproduction of dugongs, researchers think it may take more than twenty-five years for the Hervey Bay population to regain its 1988 level.

Social Behavior

Dugongs are creatures of habit. When they find a foraging area they like, they use it over and over, even when the seagrass is sparse or depleted by heavy grazing. They may stay in one spot for one to four weeks, then move to a similar area several miles away. Many dugongs, particularly those at the southern edge of their Australian range, also migrate. This behavior may be associated with seasonal

A male dugong rakes the back of another male with its tusks in an apparent dominance display.

changes in water temperature, prevailing wind and sea conditions (such as choppy, rough, or smooth waters), and the growth of preferred species of seagrass. Paul Anderson explains that blood and other birthing fluids attract predators, including sharks, prompting dugong cows to seek protective habitat, such as very shallow channels among sand bars, in which to give birth.

Dugongs live in loose social groupings whose size may fluctuate depending on food supply, reproductive behavior (such as mating and calving), environmental conditions, local and long distance movement, and hunting pressure. Scientists think that, as with manatees, the bond between a female and her calf is the only solid social relationship dugongs form. Dugongs observed in the Torres Strait between New Guinea and northern Australia by Bernard and Judith Nietschmann traveled in pairs and in small groups of three to nine animals included young, sexually mature, and old individuals. The Nietchmanns rarely saw more than twenty animals together in the Torres Strait, except for small gatherings seeking shelter from storms.

Like manatees, dugongs have daily activity cycles, which they adjust in response to tidal patterns, other environmental conditions (e.g., water temperature, high winds, or rough seas), or the level of harassment or hunting by humans. For example, where tides permit and dugongs are not threatened by humans, they may feed on and off throughout the day and night. If their access to a feeding area is affected by tide, they move in with the flood tide to feed and retreat as the tide goes out. Where dugongs are regularly hunted, they tend to feed inshore only at night and remain offshore in deeper water during the day.

Paul Anderson, after watching groups of dugongs coordinate their actions to avoid slow-moving boats and rise to the surface to investigate the passing of fast-moving boats, suggests that dugongs may work together to defend against predators. He also suggests dugongs routinely choose the same feeding sites, calving sites, and routes and destinations during seasonal migrations.

Mating Behavior and Reproduction

Both male and female dugongs become sexually mature at about ten years old, although some females mature as late as fifteen years of age. According to Helene Marsh, not all sexually mature males

A small herd of dugongs swims across a coral reef.

A female dugong swims with her calf off the coast of Australia.

are reproductively active at the same time, and periods exist when none are active. Apparently, the most males are active when the females are are active. In tropical areas of the dugong's range, breeding and calving occur on a year-round basis.

Dugongs' mating behavior resembles that of manatees. Male dugongs gather in small herds centered around a single estrous female and compete to mate with her. Tony Preen has described several phases in dugong mating behavior: a "following phase," in which up to twenty males cluster tightly around an estrous female; a "fighting phase" that includes violent splashing, rolling, and body lunges by males; and a "mounting phase," in which the victor of the fighting phase mounts the female from behind, while other males try to cling to them.

Preen, upon observing dugong behavior in Moreton Bay from a kayak, describes a typical dugong mating encounter:

"Groups of twenty or so dugongs occasionally formed within herds. They would race about energetically, jostling one another, but never really going anywhere. One cluster formed around an individual, presumably a female, that was evidently trying to outpace and outmaneuver them.

Sometimes fighting broke out within the cluster, the water seething from the surface and bodies lunged across bodies. These battles apparently determined mating rights, because mounting followed immediately.

The fighting lasted up to fifteen minutes. . . . On one of those occasions four males had mounted a female at once, clinging to her with their flippers. Meanwhile, about a dozen others circled anxiously. On the other occasions three males had attached themselves to a female.

The tension was electric as the dugongs separated. Up to sixteen agitated males, each weighing perhaps 400 kg, charged about looking for something to vent their frustration on. The atmosphere was like that in a bar when a brawl has been broken up."

Lek Displays

Paul Anderson observed some unusual sirenian social behavior among male dugongs in South Cove, an area in the eastern part of Shark Bay in western Australia. In the springs of 1988 and 1989, he watched twenty solitary male dugongs (he inferred they were males based on their behavior) defend small display territories, or leks, during their usual breeding season. This type of behavior is otherwise unknown among sirenians; although common among birds, lek displays occur among few of mammals. According to Anderson, in a classic lek, males gather and defend small display areas at a site they return to each year. There is usually little to eat, and females visit this site only to mate. This reproductive behavior contrasts sharply with the "mating herd" behavior typical in manatees and dugongs. In South Cove, says Anderson, it is possible for a male dugong in an established territory, typically a sandy area with sparse vegetation, to mate with a visiting female he has attracted by displaying and expect little interference from other males. Further, the female is not harassed by many males trying to mate with her at once.

Anderson makes a few other basic assumptions regarding the territorial dugongs of South Cove. First, because so little bottom vegetation was available, dugongs spending more than a few days on their leks must have been fasting. Second, the amount of seagrass in a territory may have determined how long a dugong could stay and may have been a measure of the quality of the territory. Finally, given that dugongs probably share the low metabolic rate of other sirenians, the defense and display activities Anderson observed must have used up extravagant amounts of energy and fat reserves. While this expenditure is uncharacteristic of dugong mating behavior, it is, Anderson states, "characteristic of male reproductive investment."

Dugongs on their leks chirped, squeaked, and barked throughout the day and night. Anderson also noted several of behaviors exclusive to resident dugongs. As they patrolled the perimeters of their territories, dugongs engaged in rooting, belly-ups, sit-ups, and bottom swims, as well as confrontations and fighting between dugongs.

When rooting, a dugong eats or gouges the bottom sediments to mark its territory. In a belly-up, a patrolling dugong rolls on its back in midwater and swims upside down for some distance.

The dugongs Anderson observed typically performed sit-ups in the center of their territory. A sit-up consists of a dugong rolling over (or doing a belly-up) and ascending vertically to the surface, coming straight out of the water with its chin tucked against its chest, facing away from the direction it had been moving. In some cases, nearly half of the dugong's body rises above the surface. It then falls backwards or sideways, somewhat like a breaching whale. After a sit-up, the dugong continues its patrol in normal swimming position, generally in the direction it had been moving before the sit-up. The South Cove dugongs usually performed sit-ups singly, but sometimes an animal would do two or more in a row. One ambitious dugong followed a belly-up with twelve consecutive sit-ups, each decreasing in height as the animal tired, until only the animal's snout broke the surface on the last sit-up.

The purpose of a sit-up is unknown. Those of the South Cove dugongs appear unrelated to the activities of an animal's neighbors. Because this movement requires so much energy, Anderson thinks it may be a display to "convey vigor, territory ownership, readiness to mate and/or quality as a potential mate." He also speculates that males may perform the sit-ups in conjunction with infrasonic sounds to attract females, although no sounds were recorded.

Anderson describes a behavior he calls "bottom swimming," in which dugongs swimming on or near the bottom, usually when patrolling the borders of their activity zones, leave a continuous black line of disturbed sediment. Nearly half of all bottom swims occurred during boundary confrontations between two male dugongs, perhaps to draw proverbial lines in the sand. A dugong engaged in a confrontation may swim back and forth parallel to his opponent (sometimes with short bursts of speed), zigzag toward his opponent, or face the other dugong while remaining stationary, rooting around on the bottom, bottom swimming, doing belly-ups, or performing sit-ups. If one dugong doesn't back away, a fight may break out. Most fights in South Cove involved only two dugongs and occurred at the boundary between neighboring territories. Sometimes a fight broke out between a resident dugong and a newcomer to the area. One fight ensued after a dugong charged into a neighboring territory and attacked its occupant with no apparent provocation.

Anderson described the thirteen fights he witnessed during his two springs at South Cove as "brief, but violent." Combatants fought below and at the water's surface, using tusks to gouge each other on the lower back near the flukes. They often raised their flukes and then slammed them on the water's surface as if to crush their opponents. In two fights, one dugong rammed the other at top speed. In one of these rammings, the impact was great enough to throw the other dugong partly out the water. In more than half the fights, the losing dugong fled at top speed, pushing up a bow wave and lunging toward the surface to breathe. On four occasions, the victor chased the fleeing dugong for up to 1,650 feet (500 m). Afterwards, both combatants appeared exhausted and out of breath, surfacing to breathe as often as every twenty seconds. By measuring the intervals between breaths, Anderson estimated the dugongs took approximately an hour to fully recover.

Anderson emphasizes that matings were rare events among the South Cove dugongs, and that they probably accounted for only a tiny fraction of the annual pregnancies in the Shark Bay dugong population. He also warns that the dugong leks in South Cove may be a unique phenomenon and that the site should be fully protected.

Cows and Calves

A dugong cow produces a single calf every three to five years, after an estimated gestation period of thirteen to fourteen months. A newborn calf is usually just under four feet (1.2 m) long and weighs about 18 pounds (30 kg). It may begin to eat seagrass soon after birth, but relies primarily on its mother's milk for up to eighteen months. Researchers believe the nutrient-rich milk allows the calf to grow quickly and therefore be less vulnerable to attack as it gains size. Because a dugong calf is entirely dependent on its mother, a calf that loses its mother is more than likely doomed. A dependent dugong calf rarely strays more than two body lengths away from its mother. To date, no account has been reported of another dugong adopting an orphaned calf, although orphaned manatee calves are often adopted by manatee cows.

The dugong cow occasionally will rest quietly while her youngster nurses, but more often will graze or surface to breathe. A manatee cow, on the other hand, generally remains still while her calf is nursing, turning slightly to one side.

When a calf is small, it often rides "piggy-back"

Dugongs with accompanying shark suckers swim over an Indo-Pacific coral reef.

on its mother. Otherwise, the flow of water around the mother's body creates suction that helps the youngster along. According to Paul Anderson, calves are less vulnerable to predators when riding on their mother's back, but he worries this behavior puts them at greater risk of being crushed by fast boats in heavily trafficked areas.

A dugong cow is protective of her calf and will risk her life to save her offspring, although she will not attack to defend it. A report from Torres Strait tells of a female dugong that lured a threatening shark into increasingly shallow water until both the cow and the shark became grounded. Although the mother was fatally mauled, the calf was able to flee to safety. In another account, a dolphin harassed a cow and calf, until a small cluster of dugongs placed themselves between the dolphin and the mother-calf pair, ending the harassment. According to Helene Marsh, aboriginal people sometimes take advantage of the mother-calf bond when hunting. If either a mother or calf is captured, the other will stay nearby and thus is easily caught.

Mortality

Human activity is a significant cause of mortality in dugongs. Dugongs drown after becoming entangled in shark nets set off beaches to protect human swimmers and in gill nets set by fishermen. Some Australian Aboriginals and Torres Strait Islanders continue to hunt dugongs legally for subsistence purposes, and poachers take dugongs in other areas. Loss of coastal habitat and increasing boat traffic are also blamed for declines in dugong populations.

Natural mortality factors include storm surges from cyclones, parasites, disease, and predation by crocodiles, killer whales, and sharks. Stonefish and stingrays have been known to give dugongs fatal surprises as they browsed on seagrass, and accounts of shark attacks on dugongs are common.

An apparently ailing female dugong was spotted by a film crew aboard the research vessel *James Scheerer* in Shark Bay on June 27, 1997. Two small tiger sharks estimated at nearly 10 feet (3 m) long were harassing the dugong, but were chased away by the crew. No other dugongs in the area responded to the ill animal's plight. An hour later, three different tiger sharks appeared, each estimated at between 13 and 16.5 feet (4–5 m) long. Within an hour, the three sharks killed and consumed the entire dugong, frequently pushing the carcass into the side of the *James Sheerer*, leaving only about a foot (30 cm) of intestine floating on the surface. Further studies by a new shark research program in Shark Bay reveal that tiger sharks may prey on dugongs with some regularity.

Dugongs have little physical capability to fight back against predators, but they may have evolved some behaviors to protect themselves during an attack. A Palauan fisherman once told Paul Anderson that when he saw a dugong attacked by a shark, it flattened itself against the bottom, attempting to protect its flippers and flukes as best it could and relying on its strong ribs and the thick skin on its back for defense. Anderson was originally skeptical about the report, but reconsidered after seeing a dugong with a healed shark bite on its back. Helene Marsh has reported dugongs with shockingly large healed wounds on the top of the head.

The important point to remember is that dugong mortality from *all* causes must remain low for dugongs to increase their numbers.

Steller's sea cow

The Steller's sea cow is named after Georg Wilhelm Steller, who first described the animal in 1741 after being shipwrecked with the Bering expedition on an uninhabited island near the Aleutian chain in the present-day Bering Sea. Fossil evidence indicates that ancestors of the Steller's sea cow lived along the Pacific Rim from Mexico to Japan for 15 million years. By all accounts, the Steller's sea cow was an immense, strange-looking animal, quite distinct from any other modern sirenians. It measured more than 25 feet (8 m) in length and may have weighed between 8,800 and 22,000 pounds (4–10 mt). It was unique among sirenians in that it lived in the cold waters of the Bering Sea, lacked teeth and finger bones, possessed a thick, corky skin, and was apparently unable to dive. It also subsisted primarily on kelp (a brown alga) rather than seagrass.

Georg Steller's written accounts of its anatomy indicate that the Steller's sea cow was internally similar to other sirenians. Its rotund body was black to blackish-brown and tapered significantly toward the whale-like flukes. A portion of the backbone that showed as a ridge beneath its hide was revealed in emaciated sea cows. Steller described the tiny head (about one-tenth the length of the body) as "somewhat [resembling] the buffalo's head, espe-

The Steller's sea cow was by all accounts an immense, strange-looking animal. This reconstruction was drawn by Pieter Folkens. Photograph © Pieter Folkens

cially as concerns the lips," with small eyes and earholes nearly lost in the wrinkles of skin on the head. Rather than teeth, the Steller's sea cow had "two broad bones (one on the upper jaw and one the lower) . . . with many crooked furrows and ridges" for crushing food. As with other sirenians, it had only pectoral flippers, but Steller describes them as "furnished with many short and densely set bristles like a scrub brush" for "[beating] the seaweed off the rocks on the bottom." Female sea cows had a teat under each flipper.

While Steller was stranded on the island, he was able to spend time observing and documenting sea cow behavior. According to Steller, they fed in large herds and grazed on the surface near shore for much of the day. When the sea cows wanted to rest, they floated on their backs in a quiet cove. They showed no fear of humans and remained in their favored feeding area no matter how many were killed by the crew. Steller noted they were resident in the waters around the island throughout the year.

According to Steller, sea cows mated in June, with only one bull pursuing one female. He did not observe "indications of an admirable intellect," but did state that "they have indeed an extraordinary love for one another, which extends so far that when one of them was cut into, all the others were intent on rescuing it and keeping it from being pulled ashore by closing a circle around it." Regarding their apparent close social ties and willingness to rescue

harpooned herd members, Steller also wrote: "Some placed themselves on the rope or tried to draw the harpoon out of its body, in which indeed they were successful several times. We also observed that a male two days in a row came to its dead female on the shore and inquired about its condition." By 1768, twenty-seven years after Georg Steller identified and named the Steller's sea cow, the unique sirenian was gone, hunted into extinction by Russian fur traders and explorers.

There is some doubt in the modern scientific community regarding the accuracy of Steller's behavioral observations, because they differ so dramatically from the loose social structure observed in living sirenians. Steller died at age thirty-seven, prior to the publication of his notes, and virtually all that is known about Steller's sea cow comes from posthumous publications that, in the words of marine mammal scientist Victor Scheffer, were "edited, copied, and translated without the help of the one man who knew the animal best."

CHAPTER 4

Sirens in Myth
and Tradition

LEFT: *A dugong flanked by golden pilot jacks
rests on a sandy bottom off the coast of Australia.*
ABOVE: *This Australian Aboriginal painting depicts dugongs
going to a shallow reef to have their babies. It was painted
in 1995 for Dr. Helene Marsh by Djanga of the
Yarrabah Community, near Cairns.*

PERHAPS NOTHING IS so intriguing about manatees and dugongs as the myths, traditions, and beliefs that surround them. Some myths, such as those describing manatees and dugongs as "sirens" or "mermaids," began as tales told by sailors, dating back to the ancient Greeks. Other stories arose from beliefs and traditions associated with the hunting of manatees and dugongs, typically by indigenous cultures in tropical zones worldwide. Universal among the stories from indigenous cultures is the reverence these people held for sirenians. In many cases manatees and dugongs supplied important food, and in some instances the ceremonies associated with hunting and feasting on these animals provided a cultural adhesive critical to the well-being of the community.

Traditional and subsistence hunting is not responsible for the overall decline of sirenian populations, as some people might like to believe. Market hunting in the nineteenth and early- to mid-twentieth centuries bears some of that burden, but the greatest impact has been caused by current human activities, including coastal development and the alteration of sirenian habitat, marine pollution, the damming of rivers, coastal commercial net fishing, and increased human use of waterways frequented by sirenians. Many of the accounts of ritual activities and customs in this chapter go back eighty years or more, and some are no longer practiced. For example, in the 1970s, some Papuan coastal tribes accustomed to a subsistence existence were encouraged by the government to change over to a cash economy. Their attitude toward much of the wildlife they hunted changed, as did many of their traditions. For the hunters from Daru, wildlife became less a source of food than a product used to buy food and other modern necessities. Hunting by this group has increased dramatically.

I have heard the mermaids
singing, each to each.
I do not think that they will sing to me.
I have seen them riding seaward on the waves
Combing the white hair of the waves blown back
when the wind blows the water white and black.
We have lingered in the chambers of the sea
By sea-girls wreathed with seaweed red and brown
Till human voices wake us, and we drown.

T.S. Eliot, from *The Love Song*
of J. Alfred Prufrock

Legends

As mentioned previously, the order Sirenia is named for the beautiful sirens of Greek mythology, whose sweet singing lured mariners to destruction on the rocks around their island. Marine mammalogists are quick to point out that manatees and dugongs are quite unlike their legendary namesakes: they do not sing, never spend time on the rocks, have never been described as "comely" or "bodacious," and it is unlikely that their charms ever lured anyone to an untimely death. Nonetheless, many scientists who pooh-pooh the sirens' spell devote virtually all of their waking moments to studying sirenians.

Classical references to mermaids or "mermen," often collectively referred to as "merfolk," may date back as far as the ancient Chaldeans, who ruled in Babylonia around 1000 B.C., and Phoenicians, who were the foremost navigators and traders of the Mediterranean by 1250 B.C. Their sea-god Ea (also known as Dagon or Oannes) was half man, half fish. The Bible mentions Dagon, as does John Milton in 1667 in Book I of *Paradise Lost*: "*Dagon* his Name; Sea Monster, upward Man and downward Fish." Among the first written accounts of mermaids was one from the Greek historian Megasthenes at the beginning of the third century B.C.E. He describes "monstere" (creatures) from the sea off Taprobanê, Sri Lanka, some of which were "in appearance like women, but instead of having locks of hair, are furnished with prickles." While unromantic, it is a relatively accurate depiction of the dugongs that frequented Indian waters during that time.

The tales told by Portuguese and Dutch sailors, however, are credited with popularizing mermaids as beautiful, seductive women-fish who wanted nothing more than to lure sailors to secluded reefs or distant seas. Mermaid stories continue today with movies such as Walt Disney Production's

With its slender build and forked flukes, this dugong could easily be mistaken for a mermaid.

A female dugong and her calf in Shark Bay, Australia. Many traditional legends tell of human mothers and daughters jumping into the ocean and becoming dugongs.

The Little Mermaid, based on a Hans Christian Andersen tale, and Hollywood's *Splash*, featuring Daryl Hannah as the lobster-munching mermaid who charms Tom Hanks into living with her forever in an undersea merfolk city.

Sirenian Creation Myths

Indigenous people tell a number of stories regarding the creation of manatees and dugongs. The Warauno of northern South America have a myth explaining the origin of manatees and tapirs. According to legend, two widowed sisters who live together quarrel fiercely. One of the sisters goes with her son to live in the forest; the other sister curses the mother and son, turning them into the first tapirs. In return, she is cursed to live in the water, and she and her unborn child become the first manatees.

Indians in Amazonas, Brazil, have a traditional belief that manatees and river dolphins are humans in a bewitched form. According to the story, the bottom of the Orinoco houses an underwater city, and people who go there, possibly by drowning, and eat the food are transformed into either manatees or river dolphins. A transformed person is called a *manari*.

In a dugong origin legend from the Trobriands, where swearing at relatives is considered highly disrespectful, a woman and her young daughter are working in the garden with the girl's uncle. After working for several hours, the daughter asks her mother to accompany her to the toilet. The mother insists that the girl ask the uncle to accompany her. The daughter asks, and her uncle consents. After the uncle and daughter return to the garden, they work for a little while more. Then, the girl asks her mother to use the toilet again. Once more, the mother insists the girl ask her uncle. When the girl asks her uncle, he becomes furious and tells her with foul language to use the toilet on her own. She runs back to her mother and tells what her uncle has said. The mother is shocked at the uncle's words and leads her daughter from the garden down to the sea. When they reach the water's edge, they continue walking into the sea until their grass skirts float loose and spread over the water's surface. In the sea, the mother and her daughter turn into a female dugong and her calf.

As late as the 1970s, hunters from the Trobriands carried grass skirts so that dugongs, thinking the skirts were those left on the water in the legend, would be unafraid and thus easier to catch. When a dugong was caught, the hunters wrapped the grass skirts over its nostrils until it suffocated.

In many Papuan villages, dugong hunters are not allowed to sleep with their wives for two weeks before a hunt. This story by Alpha Eko of Gabagaba village tells why:

Long ago a young couple got married. Soon the wife was expecting a baby. Near the time for her to give birth she told her husband to go to the garden to get some bananas to eat. She cleaned the house and on the way to take the rubbish to the sea, she felt that the baby was soon to be born. She hurried down to the sea and gave birth, not to a human baby, but to a Dugong. The woman became frightened of her husband because of this and returned every day to the beach to feed her infant without telling her husband.

After a few weeks the husband started to wonder about his wife and one day followed her to the beach and saw her feeding the baby Dugong. He ran to the house and got his spear and ran back to the beach and speared the Dugong. The woman let the baby go from her breast, but before the baby Dugong swam away, it said to the man, "Father you have tried to spear me, so I am no longer your

This painting of Torres Strait Islanders roasting a dugong in primitive style was created in 1979 by Aboriginal artist Goobalathalden, also known as Dick Roughsey to field anthropologists. From the collection of Dr. Helene Marsh.

daughter and if you wish to see or catch me, do not sleep with your wife for two weeks. Then come looking for me." With this the Dugong swam away.

Traditional Beliefs and Taboos

Many native cultures regarded manatees and dugongs highly for their food value, and a fascinating array of beliefs and rituals were involved in virtually all aspects of hunting, butchering, and feasting on sirenians. Perhaps the most intriguing examples come from the Rama Indians of Nicaragua and the Mälnkänidji of Cape York Peninsula, Australia.

During 1969 and 1970, anthropologist Franklin O. Loveland spent several months with the Rama Indians of southeastern Nicaragua. He

An Antillean manatee floats over a seagrass bed off the coast of Belize in Central America. These manatees have been hunted by people for thousands of years.

obtained a great deal of information regarding the role of both the manatee and the tapir in the Rama belief system. Much of what follows was gleaned from his fascinating essay "Tapirs and Manatees: Cosmological Categories and Social Process Among the Rama Indians." The Rama lived in small forest settlements, with easy access to rivers, an estuarine lagoon, and the Caribbean Sea. The Rama, whose name for the Antillean manatee of their region was *palpah*, believed the animal was intelligent and had an acute sense of hearing. They refrained from talking about the location of the manatee or the charms they were carrying for fear the animal would hear them and be forewarned of their hunting plans. They considered the manatee symbolic of the cultural world, representing quiet, social order, solidarity in the community, and resources of the water. In contrast, the tapir was associated with nature, asociality, and disorder. When hunting a manatee, a number of taboos were observed to increase the chances of success, while little symbolic significance was attached to hunting tapir. When a tapir was killed, no rituals were involved and no feast was held. However, if a manatee was killed, the butchering and distribution of meat was done with great care, and the feast that followed was an important event in the community.

The Rama performed several rituals for the preservation of manatees and successful hunts. To ensure the continued presence of manatees, they always returned manatee bones to the lagoon where the animal was killed. For success on future hunts, manatee meat was roasted and eaten immediately after the kill, and the hunters bathed in the animal's blood. The Rama also believed that manatees in the lagoon were protected by a large whale who could reverse the current and would devour anyone who tried to harm the manatees.

The striker, or person who threw the harpoon, was held in high esteem by the community. He was not allowed to eat the meat of the animal he killed, unless it was his first manatee, in which case he was given a piece of meat from above the heart to guarantee he would kill more. The striker was given the tail and breastbone, which he in turn would give away; he also received the ear bones, which he kept

A Torres Strait Islander hurls himself overboard in his effort to harpoon a dugong. Photograph © Ben Cropp Productions/ Innerspace Visions

*Torres Strait Islanders on Boigu Island perform a traditional dance with harpoons that reenacts a dugong hunt. Photograph ©
Ben Cropp Productions/Innerspace Visions*

as a charm for future hunts. The ear bone was used by the hunter as "magic" to prevent the manatee from hearing him. A striker would not share the techniques or charms he used when hunting. According to Loveland, at one time an excellent woman striker lived in the Rama community. By 1970, however, only a handful of manatee hunters remained and all were men.

Halfway around the world and more than fourty years earlier, anthropologist Donald Thomson from the University of Melbourne spent several months with a group of fishing and seafaring tribes on the east coast of the Cape York Peninsula in northern Australia. These tribes, known by anthropologists as the Kawadji, the people of the east, called themselves Mälnkänidji, the sandbeachmen (*belonging to the sandbeach*). Thomson and his wife lived with the sandbeachmen in 1928; his excellent paper, *The Dugong Hunters of Cape York*, is the source of the following information on these people and their traditions.

Men of one of the smaller sandbeach tribes, the Yintjingga, were renowned for their abilities as canoemen and dugong hunters, their prowess with the long harpoon, and the potency of their dugong magic. Thomson described them as a tribe near extinction in 1928, but according to Helene Marsh, they have survived, although they have given up their traditional hunting techniques. The Yintjingga harpooners used magical bundles, which were simply lumps of beeswax called *mänkä* obtained from inland Aboriginals. On the afternoon preceding a hunt, the harpooner, or *wotadji* (dugong man, or *belonging to the dugong*) would discreetly perform a ceremony in which he warmed the lump of *mänkä* over a fire and pressed it just above his navel two or three times. When he hunted the next day, magic would cause the dugong or sea turtle he encountered to be sluggish and easily harpooned and secured. Apart from that rite, a dugong man might also speak or chant a spell that in English the natives called "singing the dugong." *Wotadji* whose hair and beards were gray were honored with the cognomen *Tjilbo*, the gray one. Dugongs were typically hunted during the day, but during certain seasons they were hunted by moonlight. The Yintjingga believed that hunting in the moonlight caused of premature grayness, but graying early did not earn a young dugong man the title of *Tjilbo*.

Luck was a major factor in bringing in a dug-

ong, and many things could cause bad luck to a *wotadji*. No one was permitted to burn the hide or remains of a dugong. Bones were collected and thrown into the river or estuary, to be gathered periodically and placed in neatly arranged piles until required for a human burial, where they adorned the top of the grave. According to Thomson, after a hunt "[h]air clippings, or any personal belongings, particularly objects impregnated with body sweat, were also carefully collected and thrown into water, never into a fire, where they can no longer be used by an enemy to work evil magic against the owner," specifically the *wotadji*. *Wotadji* were forbidden to touch or carry the body or bones of a dead person or to use dugong blood to dye the shafts of spears.

Among the Yintjingga, the butchering of a dugong was a social event carried out according to rigid tradition. This custom still holds true for many of the dugong hunters of the Torres Strait. The animal is carved according to a prescribed pattern and meat is distributed without cost throughout the community. The best cuts of meat typically go to the butcher and/or harpooner and crew before the remainder is shared. According to anthropologists Bernard and Judith Nietschmann, Torres Strait Islanders distinguish between at least fourty-five different cuts of dugong meat. A total of twenty-seven different terms are used to describe the dugongs themselves to differentiate sex, size, reproductive status, and relative health and food-quality. The Nietschmanns also point out that for Torres Strait Islanders, "hunting is more than a subsistence trait,

After a successful hunt, Torres Strait Islanders butcher a dugong according to a prescribed pattern and meat is distributed without cost throughout the community. Photograph © Ben Cropp Productions/Innerspace Visions

a means to acquire meat, or an aberrant relic of past times; it is a way of life. Around marine hunting and the pursuit and capture of large herbivores revolves a complex system of logic and knowledge, environmental perception, social expectations and responsibilities, and the resilient roots of Islander myths and legends."

Not all native cultures valued sirenians as important entities. Some aboriginal communities to the west of Cape York Peninsula have never hunted dugongs. In Cameroon, West Africa, a Yale University student conducting research in the late 1980s was told by Akwen fishermen that West African manatees live in caves, are dangerous, and can drown people. In the village of Akpasang, some hunter/fishermen believe that manatees receive their power from the devil. In a 1933 story for *Natural History Magazine,* Guy Dollman described the fear of manatees among certain tribes along the Niger River:

Mr. Woods in his report on this animal

Amazonian manatees have long been a preferred meat source, in part because they are relatively easy to catch and provide a great deal of meat that is slow to decay, an important factor in the tropics. Photograph © Ken Lucas/Planet Earth Pictures.

states that to many tribes the manatee is "ju-ju." The Abos believe that it is certain death even to see one, and the same belief seems to exist amongst the Asaba and other tribes inhabiting the banks of the Niger. All the regular hunters of the manatee would appear to be Haussas, and when a carcass of one is being towed in, a warning drum commences to beat a special rhythm, which continues until the beast has been cut up. If killed at a distance or after a prolonged struggle, it sometimes happens that it is evening before the body arrives at the bank of the river, and then it is necessary for the drumming to continue all night until the carcass is cut up the next morning.

Even the relatively diminutive, exceedingly shy Amazonian manatee was feared by some tribes. According to Alexander von Humboldt, who explored the Amazon region from 1799 to 1804, the Piaroas of the Meta River (an Orinocan tributary) said that their people invariably died when they ate manatee meat. Luis Marden, on assignment in Guatemala for *National Geographic* in the 1940s, wrote that "Livingston people assured me solemnly that 'anyone struck with a manatee crop [whip], however lightly, will shrivel up and die. Just touch someone with it in anger, and soon he is a husk, just like a mummy.'"

Traditional and Commercial Uses

Sirenians have been hunted by humans for thousands of years. Dugong hide is believed to have been used in biblical times for the cover or "Outer Fly" of the Tabernacle, the portable sanctuary in which the Jews carried the Ark of the Covenant through the desert. People living along the coast of the Red Sea long used dugong hide for the soles of sandals. Archaeologists have found worked manatee bones, including carved figurines representing humans and a carved canoe, among spear heads and pottery rings on what is believed to be an ancient Mayan fishing site in Belize. As with whales and seals, virtually every imaginable part of the manatee and dugong has been put to practical use by humans at one time or another.

Sirenians are hunted primarily for their meat and fat. Manatee meat was preferred over beef by

A manatee and her calf feed on turtle grass off the coast of Belize, where they are protected from hunting by law, although poaching does occur.

A dugong rolls around on the sand bottom, possibly in an attempt to dislodge remoras.

European explorers, and Aborigines and Torres Strait Islanders still hold dugong meat in higher esteem than even the highly valued meat of the green turtle. The abundance of meat and fat from a manatee or dugong has historically made these animals valuable sources of protein to native cultures and European sailors. Manatee and dugong meat may vary in color and taste like pork, beef, or veal—depending on what part of the body the meat is taken from—due to differences in the amounts of myoglobin (a protein) in the muscle. Both the meat and fat are somewhat resistant to spoilage, which increases their value in tropical climates. European explorers raved about the taste of manatee flesh, and as Spanish missionaries and soldiers pushed ever deeper into Central and South America, the Catholic Church conveniently decreed the manatee a fish, making it fit to eat anytime, including Fridays, without sin. (Moslems reacted similarly, prizing dugong flesh as a pork substitute.)

Jose de Acosta, upon visiting the Windward Islands in 1588, had some qualms about the manatee, considering it "a strange kind of fish [which] when I did eat of it at St. Dominque on a friday, I had some scruple, not for that which is spoken, but for that in colour and taste it was like unto morsels of veale." According to one seventeenth-century account of the "fish," "The meat is very fat and tasty. His tail is like bacon, without any lean meat, which they melt as pork fat. It is used as butter that can be used like lard but with a better taste. The fish meat, cooked with vegetables, has the same taste as beef. It keeps the salt better, when seasoned, it looks and tastes like pork meat. If cured, it turns very red and will taste as extremely good pork meat after cooked."

The Carib consumed manatee flesh to cure indigestion caused by eating too many crabs, which were their primary food. In Venezuela, manatee meat was eaten fresh or salted, or was used medicinally, believed by some to be a remedy for syphilis and dental problems. In Brazil, manatee meat was valued more than beef and often boiled in its own fat to form a concoction called *mixira*. *Mixira* was tinned or stored in clay pots, where it would keep for several months.

On the Torres Strait Islands between Australia and Papua New Guinea, dugong meat remains essential fare at Islander feasts held to commemorate baptisms, weddings, funerals, and tombstone open-ings. Celebrations may draw as many as 1,000 people and require up to twelve dugongs. In the absence of dugong meat, green turtles are used.

Manatee and dugong blubber was occasionally eaten raw, but generally it was rendered into oil for cooking, medicinal uses, or use in lanterns. Some accounts state that as much as 220 pounds (100 kg) of fat could be carved from a single large manatee. In the eighteenth century, the French considered manatee oil as sweet as butter and sent it from Guyana to Cayenne, where it was incorporated into soups, fricassees, and pastries. In the Amazon region, manatee oil was mixed with pitch to caulk boats. In Venezuela, oil was used to relieve back-aches and arthritis, and in Cameroon intestinal fat from the West African manatee is still rubbed on one's body to soothe aching joints.

Dugong oil is said to be similar to cod liver oil (but much more palatable), and up to eight gallons may be rendered from an average adult animal. It is thought by some indigenous groups to cure everything from tuberculosis to joint pain.

Other parts of sirenians have been used for a variety of purposes. Manatee skin has been boiled and mixed with rum as a cure for asthma; dried for use as whips, wrappings, mats, and shields "strong enough to resist arrows and even shot"; and cooked to an ash to be used as a preventative against diarrhea. Dugong tears are sold by fishermen in parts

The historic uses of dugong parts are various and inventive, including dugong hide covering the Tabernacle, dugong oil to cure tuberculosis, and dugong tears as an aphrodisiac.

of Asia as an aphrodisiac, and in parts of Africa, the consumption of male manatee genitalia is believed to help overcome impotence. Sirenian bones and teeth have been utilized as fishing hooks and lures, musical instruments, utensils, scraping tools, nut crushers, limesticks, jewelry, and garden charms (to better grow vegetables and pigs). Burned to ash, they find applications in treating insect bites, combating lung ailments, curing ulcers, and providing relief for women during menstruation.

The inner ear bones, or "stones," of manatees and dugongs have traditionally been used—and may still be used in some areas—for their magical or medicinal properties. Manatee stones were used as charms against witchcraft in the Yucatán and by the Miskito Indians of Nicaragua to prevent bad luck. In Panama and Guatemala, ear bones brought relief from painful childbirth. Early English travelers valued the stones as a remedy for colic and dysentery "when beat small and drunk fasting"—that is, when the ear bones are beaten to a small size and ingested on an empty stomach. In Venezuela, most remedies involving ear bones were applied to children. Children who wore an amulet made from ear bones were protected against diarrhea and teething pain. Among the Warauno, children could be cured of illnesses caused by bad people who stared at them with "an evil eye," but only if the boys wore the ear bones from a female manatee and the girls wore those of a male. Among the Chinese, the ear bones of dugongs are prized when finely powdered and taken to cleanse the kidneys.

Although all three species of manatee and the dugong have been subjected to past hunting pressure, some on a commercial basis, the exploitation of the dugong and the Amazonian manatee has been the best documented. Killing and processing dugongs for their oil provided a profitable commercial enterprise in Australia from the 1850s until dugongs received protection from commercial exploitation in the late 1960s. Meat was salted down and sold as a type of bacon. Fat was rendered and used in medicinal oils. Rib bones were burned and used as charcoal for sugar refining. Dugong hide was turned into coach brakes, glue, or thick leather for saddles. Tusks were polished for use as handles on meat carvers. The entire Moreton Bay dugong population is believed to have been destroyed by a cottage industry that exploited them for their oil from the mid-1800s to the 1940s. Fortunately, this population has recovered.

Brazil was the hub of the export of manatee products from the Amazon region for more than 150 years. From the 1780s to about 1925, the only manatee product common in Amazonian commerce was *mixira*, a food formed by boiling manatee meat in its own fat. Nearly 462,000 pounds (210,000 kg) entered the Belém market between 1876 and 1915. From 1935 to 1954, manatee hides were exported to southern Brazil and elsewhere to make heavy-duty leather. From 1954 to the banning of manatee hunting in 1973, manatees were again heavily exploited for meat. According to biologist Miriam Marmontel, *mixira* is still a delicacy in Brazil and commands high prices in towns. Although Daryl Domning states that manatee products never made up more than a small fraction of a percent of the Amazon trade, between 4,000 and 7,000 manatees are estimated to have been slaughtered annually—in addition to an unrecorded number killed for subsistence purposes—during the peak years of hide and meat production.

Subsistence Hunting and Its Demise

The array of hunting methods used by native tribes to dispatch manatees and dugongs could itself fill a book. Torres Strait Islanders harpooned dugongs from portable hunting platforms built over seagrass beds, until they switched to canoes in the early 1900s. Around that same time, the Kiwai people from Daru and the adjacent coastal areas of Papua

An Amazonian manatee is butchered by people living along the Jurua' River. Photograph © Miriam Marmontel

TOP: *Ivory Coast fishermen capture a West African manatee with a trap net. Various types of traps are used to catch West African manatees, including the fence trap, in which a hunter drops a trap door behind a manatee that is feeding among mangroves. Another is the spear trap, used in the Pujehun and Bonthe districts of Sierra Leone, in which a manatee moves through an opening between two posts and pushes against a net that crosses the opening. This drives a spear, propelled by the force of a heavy log behind it, deep into the animal, effectively tethering it until the hunters arrive. Photograph © J. Powell*
BOTTOM: *A manatee trap, Ivory Coast, Africa. Photograph © J. Powell*

An Amazonian manatee feeds on vegetation at the edge of a river. Photograph © Fernando Trujillo/Innerspace Visions

New Guinea began harpooning dugongs from *motomotos*, two-masted, double-hulled, sailing canoes. Most dugong hunting now is done with a harpoon from canoes or aluminum dinghies equipped with outboard motors. In West Africa, manatees are either speared from a platform, using fresh-cut grass as bait, or captured in nets or traps. In Florida, the Timucuan Indians hunted manatees from canoes, lassoed them, and then drove a sharpened stick or crude harpoon into their noses to stop their breathing and keep them from sinking out of reach. In the Amazon basin, manatees were shot with arrows, shot with poison darts from a blow gun, or harpooned.

The unusual method Orinocan Indians used to hunt manatees was first recorded in 1791 by Jesuit explorer José Gumilla. They used a double-barbed harpoon tied to their canoes by a rope of manatee hide. A paddler and a harpooner manned the canoe. Once the hunters harpooned and killed a manatee, they leaped into the water, holding onto the sides of the canoe and then tilting it so that it filled with water. The canoe was then easily pushed under the manatee and emptied of water by using bailers they wore on their heads as hats. Once the canoe had risen sufficiently with its load, the hunters paddled away. During his trip to the Amazon basin, Alexander von Humboldt described a similar method used by another tribe. Most indigenous people hunting with harpoons used a breakaway head tethered to a long line and some sort of float to track their quarry's movements.

In the Caribbean, manatees were traditionally harpooned. The Spanish used crossbows. The Carib Indians utilized perhaps the most creative and implausible means of catching manatees. A large species of remora, or "suckerfish" as they are commonly known (scientists believe it was *Echeneis*), was

A Kiwai harpooner hurls himself off the bow of his motu motu *(sail canoe) to plunge a harpoon deep into the back of a dugong. A* motu motu *requires a large crew, including a helmsman, dugong spotter, harpooner, and crew to operate the sails. A master hunter typically orchestrates the hunt and directs the crew. The* motu motu *is traditionally constructed with charms, including flowers and echidna quills, sealed into the bow piece. If the* motu motu *crew was successful, they raise a flag as they approach their village, signaling someone on shore to blow a conch horn to summon the people to the beach. One dugong will provide enough food for the entire village. Photograph © D. Parer and E. Parer-Cook/AUSCAPE*

A female dugong and her calf swim together in Shark Bay, Australia.

captured when young, possibly kept tethered in a shallow pool, and fed by hand. Once the fish, or "pegador" (catcher), grew large enough, it was secured by a line at the base of the tail and taken fishing for manatees, sea turtles, and larger fish. The fisherman would spot his prey, release the fish in the direction of the intended target, and the remora apparently rocketed away to attach itself to the unsuspecting animal. The remora and prey were then steadily (and probably very quietly) hauled in by the line. Once the prey was secured, the remora released its hold and reattached itself to the side of the boat. According to Raymond Gilmore in *Handbook of South American Indians*, "it is certain the natives generally prized their 'captives' [semi-domesticated remoras], spoke to them in endearing terms, and rewarded them with meat after each successful hunt." Several researchers observed this hunting practice; none believed the others until they had seen it for themselves.

Although laws protect manatees and dugongs in most places they are found, poaching for subsistence and sale at market still occurs regularly (with the exception of the Florida manatee), but apparently with decreasing frequency. Manatee meat in some places in West Africa and South America is sold openly in markets, and in East Africa and Asia dugongs are caught incidentally in nets and taken for food. As late as 1986, there was significant commercial demand by the military for Amazonian manatee meat in Ecuador. Most hunters know that killing manatees and dugongs is largely prohibited, but continue because the potential profit greatly outweighs the chance of significant punishment.

A case in point is the gruesome discovery in 1995 by Bob Bonde and a team of conservationists of at least thirty-five manatee carcasses at eleven remote sites in Belize. Bonde thinks the sites were used by Guatemalan fishermen who killed the manatees in Belize's Port Honduras, butchered them at processing sites at night, and then transported the meat back to Guatemala to be sold at market. According to Bonde, manatee meat on the Guatemalan market goes for $2.50 to $5.00 a pound, and poachers can carve 400 to 500 pounds of meat from a large manatee.

The reasons for limiting or altogether banning hunting are clear. Sirenians reproduce slowly and cannot recover quickly after a population crashes due to hunting or a natural calamity. According to

Helene Marsh, between 22,000 and 44,000 dugongs must exist in the Torres Strait region to sustain an annual harvest of 500 to 1,000 animals. Rough estimates of the dugong population suggest that more than 40,000 dugongs may indeed live in the Torres Strait. However, Marsh cautions that no accurate catch numbers, population estimates, or life history parameters exist, and an apparent abundance of dugongs should not lead to an unlimited harvest. According to Marsh's calculations, if a herd maintains healthy reproduction—every cow over age ten producing one calf every three years—the population still would be unlikely to increase at more than 5 percent a year. These figures indicate that for a regional population of 200 dugongs to remain stable, no more than five cows a year can be killed by humans.

Many native cultures respect the law and understand why sirenians can no longer be hunted. Some tribes, such as the Siona in Ecuador, initiated self-imposed bans to conserve the remaining animals. Others, such as the Mornington Island Aboriginals, avoid killing pregnant female dugongs—which are traditionally viewed as the fattest and most desireable—as a conservation measure. Aboriginal communities elsewhere have agreed to limiting their hunting to certain areas, leaving other places as refuges for dugongs. Some mainland Aboriginal communities have turned to hunting wild cattle, buffalo, and pigs to take the pressure off dugongs. All of these measures offer hope for the future survival of sirenians and their place in the lives of native cultures.

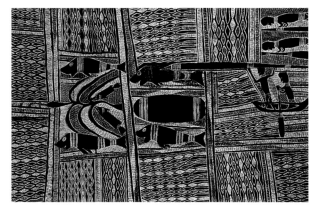

In this example of Australian Aboriginal bark art, created in a traditional motif by Marrirra Marawili of the Madarrpa Clan, Yirritja Moiety, hunters successfully spear a dugong from a canoe.

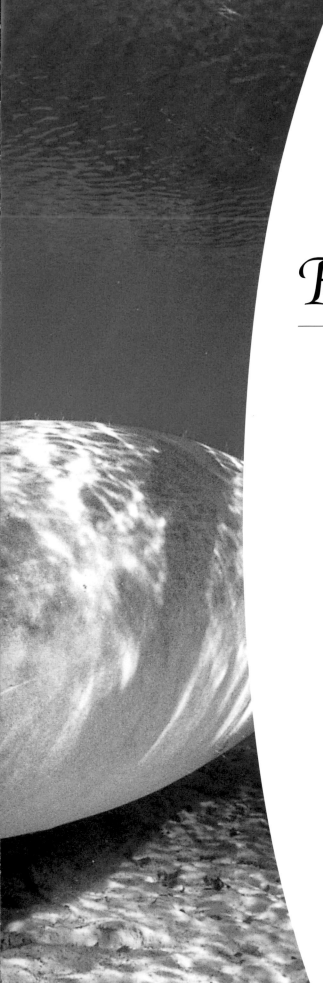

CHAPTER 5

Finding Sanctuary

LEFT: *Two manatees play at Blue Spring State Park, Florida. Approximately 2,600 Florida manatees remain in the wild.*
ABOVE: *Two snorkelers approach a Florida manatee in a spring near Crystal River.*

MANATEES AND DUGONGS have few predators, yet in most parts of the world, their populations continue to decline. Natural mortality claims sirenians every year, but it is the high percentage of deaths resulting from humans and human-related activity that is so alarming. Some 35 percent of all manatee deaths in Florida in 1998 were directly attributable to humans. What is unforgivable is that many of the human-caused deaths are preventable. In other parts of the world, neither the total number of sirenian deaths from all causes nor the percentage of deaths caused by humans is known.

Why do people have such an impact on sirenians? Manatees and dugongs are restricted to coastal areas and rivers where human activity is concentrated. They are slow to reproduce. They have no real physical defenses and no defensive behavior except to swim away. Although sirenians have contended with a low level of natural mortality throughout their evolution, their

In Australia, killing dugongs is prohibited except for harvesting by certain indigenous tribes.

slow reproduction and lack of physical defense and behavior are thought by scientists to be an outcome of the lack of a significant predatory presence—at least for the four living species. We are the primary predators of manatees and dugongs—even if we never pick up a rifle or harpoon—armed with boats, floodgates and salinity barriers, nets, marine refuse, dams, and the ability to alter and destroy coastal habitat. Countless examples exist of animal species evolving in the absence of predators and then, after humans arrive (with associated exotic baggage, including cats, pigs, goats, chickens, snakes, monkeys, and mongooses), soon becoming extinct. Dodo, Tasmanian wolf, passenger pigeon, New Zealand laughing owl, Jamaican iguana, Guam rail, Laysan honeycreeper, Cuban yellow bat, Antarctic wolf, Steller's sea cow—these are only a few names in the litany of animal extinctions caused directly or indirectly by humans within the last three hundred years. Are manatees and dugongs next?

A common question asked by politicians, developers, boating lobbyists, and representatives of other groups inconvenienced by regulatory complications is "How many of these animals do we really

need?" Obviously no moral answer exists to such a question, but Miriam Marmontel, Stephen Humphrey, and Thomas O'Shea address this issue in their controversial 1996 article for Conservation Biology. Using the layers of growth in the inner ear bones of 1,212 carcasses obtained throughout Florida from 1976 to 1991, Marmontel and her colleagues were able to obtain age specific data on the reproduction and survival of the Florida manatee.

Their population viability analysis indicates that the short term Florida manatee population is stable, but the long term population is threatened 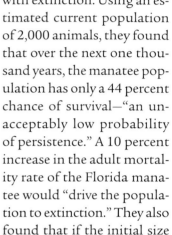 with extinction. Using an estimated current population of 2,000 animals, they found that over the next one thousand years, the manatee population has only a 44 percent chance of survival—"an unacceptably low probability of persistence." A 10 percent increase in the adult mortality rate of the Florida manatee would "drive the population to extinction." They also found that if the initial size of the population is doubled from 2,000 to 4,000, the probability of survival increases by 50 percent, indicating that a higher initial population leads to a greater chance of ultimate survival. Given the estimated 1996 minimum population of 2,600 manatees, which is 30 percent more than the study's base population, probability of survival creeps up to about 57 percent—still precarious for a species to survive over the next millennium.

Although the World Conservation Union suggests that "one hundred years is realistic in terms of prediction accuracy and legal expectations," Marmontel and her colleagues argue that "a millennium is a more appropriate time scale to evaluate population trends and enable adaptive and evolutionary processes to operate." (A similar scale was adopted by scientists for grizzly bears, which also have long life spans and are slow to reproduce.) The problem is that to the human mind one thousand years is an inconceivably long time, and the average person has difficulty fathoming the necessity of implementing measures now that are designed to increase a species' probability of maintaining a viable population over the course of a millennium.

A Florida manatee rests in Blue Spring State Park, Florida, where it is protected under the United States Endangered Species Act and Marine Mammal Protection Act.

This Florida manatee's fluke has been mutilated by a boat propeller.

Another important note: Thirteen coastal counties were targeted by Florida in 1989 as "key" to mortality-reduction efforts through local boat-speed zoning; Marmontel, Humphrey, and O'Shea point out that only one additional adult manatee death in each of these counties (fourteen to seventeen manatee deaths statewide) would be enough to increase the mortality rate by 10 percent and nudge the Florida manatee toward extinction. According to the U.S. Fish and Wildlife Service, between 1976 and 1997, the number of manatee carcasses collected has increased by an average of 6.3 percent each year. Things are not improving for manatees.

Marine mammalogists are concerned about how well dugongs can survive in the face of continued human-related losses in shark nets around popular beaches in Australia, incidental capture in fishermen's nets throughout the dugong's range, land use practices that cause habitat loss, and continued subsistence hunting by Aborigines and Torres Strait Islanders in northern Australia and Papua New Guinea. According to computer simulations, if dugongs are to continue to survive, more

than 95 percent of the adult females alive at the beginning of a year must be alive at the end of the year. Based on this information, no more than a 2 percent mortality of adult females from all human impacts can be sustained each year. Further, if dugongs do not find enough to eat because of habitat deterioration, the females will probably produce fewer calves and the percentage of sustainable mortality will be even less.

Human-related mortality

Collisions with watercraft are by far the primary human-related cause of death in Florida manatees. In a typical collision, a manatee swimming at or near the surface is struck by a boat or ship and is either crushed by the hull or lacerated by the propellers. Most deaths result from blunt impact by the boat hull rather than from propeller cuts. In 1997, out of a total of 242 manatee mortalities, 55 deaths (23 percent) were deemed watercraft-related. In 1998, out of a total of 231 manatee mortalities, the number of watercraft-related deaths rose to 66, or 35 percent of the year's total mortality. The actual number of manatees killed by boats may be higher since most recovered carcasses are too badly decomposed to determine cause of death. The U.S. Fish and Wildlife Service reports that over the last two decades, deaths caused by watercraft strikes increased at 7.1 percent per year. This statistic is alarming because it means that watercraft-related deaths continue to rise despite increased efforts to educate boaters about manatees and the establishment of manatee speed zones in areas frequented by manatees. Mortality from boat strikes is usually highest in Brevard County in the Cape Canaveral area on Florida's east-central coast.

An analysis of 406 manatees killed by watercraft found that the majority (55 percent) were killed by impact and a substantial number (39 percent) were killed by propeller cuts. Most propeller wounds were on the manatees' backs and sides rather than their heads, suggesting the animals were diving to avoid a collision when they were struck. Propeller guards do little to prevent boat injury to manatees. Overall, the wounds suggested that most lethal propeller wounds were caused by mid-sized or large boats, but that impact injuries appear to be caused by fast-moving small to mid-sized boats. Because manatees may have difficulty hearing boat engines, researchers at Florida Atlantic University are developing a high-speed sonic beam that would be mounted on the boat's engine. The beam would alert manatees to boat presence earlier than the engine noise, giving the animals more time to move away.

Part of the problem is the number of boats on the water. Bureau of Vessels and Titling records show that for the 1996 to 1997 boating season, more than 795,000 boats were registered in Florida, 95 percent of which were for pleasure purposes. Of these registered boats, 85,000 were personal watercraft, which are often operated at high speed in fragile, shallow areas. More than 300,000 boats registered in other states are launched on Florida's waters each year as well, swelling the total number of boats plying state water at any given time to about 1.1 million. That's about 400 boats to every manatee. The number of boats on the water will only increase as the human population continues to grow. As the number of boats increases, the likelihood of manatees being hit will also rise.

Floodgates and canal locks are yet another source of human-related manatee mortality. Several manatees die each year after becoming trapped in water control structures and navigation locks. In some cases, manatees are crushed when doors close on them. Sometimes they drown when they are pinned against narrow door openings by rushing water. Since scientists began counting and evaluating manatee mortalities in 1974, more than 130 manatees have been killed by water control structures. Dade County, which has many of these structures, accounts for the majority of these deaths in recent years.

Each year, a few additional manatees die from poaching and vandalism, entrapment in shrimp nets and other fishing gear, entrapment in water pipes, and ingestion of marine debris. In 1997, 8 manatees died from these causes, the highest recorded number since 1979. Between 1976 and 1991, deaths in this category have ranged from 2 percent to 5 percent of the total mortality. Incidents of poaching or vandalism are fairly rare in Florida, and the state's ban on certain types of net fishing reduces the chance that manatees will be entangled in nets. Marine debris, however, remains a threat to manatees. Researchers Cathy Beck and Nelio Barros found monofilament fishing line, plastic bags, string, twine, rope, fish hooks, wire, paper, synthetic sponges, stockings, and rubber bands in the stomachs of 14.4 percent of 439 manatee carcasses salvaged between 1978 and 1986. Discarded monofilament line, the most common debris found, and rope (such as from commercial crab traps) are frequently

This manatee's flipper is entangled in line from a crab trap.
Photograph © Sirenia Project

A Florida manatee calf flosses on an anchor line near Crystal River.

discovered wrapped around flippers of wild, living manatees. Tightly wrapped lines act like a tourniquet, cutting off the supply of blood to the flippers and causing the limbs to die; entanglement in lines can easily be fatal to a manatee. It is now illegal in Florida to discard monofilament fishing line or netting into the water.

In total, seventy-one manatee deaths in Florida due to human-related causes were tallied in 1997. In less than twenty-five years, more than 1,500 manatees—more than half of the current estimated population of Florida manatees—died in Florida as a result of human activity.

For dugongs, human-related mortality data is available only for Australia. However, the data are sketchy, mainly because scientists must cover a much greater area than in Florida. According to Helene Marsh, dugongs in Australia are affected by hunting, fishing, coastal development, and unsustainable agricultural practices. Mortality statistics, which are collected by the Queensland Shark Control Program, show that since shark nets were introduced in the 1960s, nearly a thousand dugongs have died in shark nets in northeastern Australia.

Most of these shark net entanglements and resulting deaths occurred in the early years of the program. In the early 1990s, after the program was modified and steps were taken to reduce the mortality of protected wildlife, the number of dugongs captured in shark nets in eastern Queensland dropped dramatically.

Subsistence hunting continues to draw from the dugong population in the Torres Strait. Helene Marsh and her colleagues estimate that from 1991 to 1993, more than 1,200 dugongs were caught each year, a few of which were sold illegally at the Daru market in Papua New Guinea. Marsh has stated repeatedly that she is not certain if the dugong population in the Torres Strait region can withstand such a harvest, particularly because no accurate estimate of the region's total dugong population exists, and because the life history of that population is not fully understood.

Conserving Sirenians

Given the grim mortality statistics, the critical need for sirenian conservation is easy to see. Manatees and dugongs are protected by law in virtually every

Dugongs and other large marine animals are often caught in nets set off Australian beaches to protect swimmers from sharks, like this great white. Photograph © Ron and Valerie Taylor/Innerspace Visions

country they inhabit. Protection ranges from international treaties to local edicts, but enforcement of these laws varies considerably from country to country.

International Protection

The Convention on International Trade in Endangered Species of Wild Fauna and Flora provides an international structure for regulating trade in species that are, or may soon be, threatened with extinction. The United States and 102 other countries are signatories to this agreement. Species currently threatened with extinction are listed under Appendix I of the Convention. Those species that could become threatened if trade is not regulated are listed under Appendix II. The dugong is listed under Appendix I throughout its range, except in Australia, where it appears under Appendix II. Both subspecies of the West Indian manatee and the Amazonian manatee are listed under Appendix I, and the West African manatee appears under Appendix II.

All three species of manatees and the dugong receive protection in U.S. Territorial waters under the United States Endangered Species Act and Marine Mammal Protection Act. The Endangered Species Act (ESA) protects any species of fish or wildlife currently endangered or threatened with extinction from being taken (defined as "to harass, harm, pursue, hunt, shoot, wound, kill, trap, capture, or collect, or attempt to engage in any such conduct"). Under the ESA, any endangered species, its parts, or any products made from that species, may not be imported, exported, possessed, or sold, whether within or outside of the United States. The ESA also requires the designation of critical habitat essential to the conservation of a listed species, including adequate area for the species to expand its range and recover to a healthy population level. The Marine Mammal Protection Act (MMPA) makes it illegal, with certain exceptions (including subsistence hunting), to kill, injure, capture, or harass any species of marine mammal, or to attempt any of these activities in U.S. waters. The MMPA also makes it unlawful to import marine mammals or related products into the United States.

West African manatees are protected under

Class A of the African Convention for the Conservation of Nature and Natural Resources, originally signed in 1969 by thirty-eight African countries.

Protection of Florida Manatees

In Florida, government efforts to conserve manatees began in 1892, when the Florida legislature enacted manatee protection laws after extensive hunting by settlers earlier in the century significantly reduced the population. Federal protection for manatees came in 1972 and 1973 with the passage of the MMPA and ESA, respectively. The state of Florida followed these acts with the Florida Manatee Sanctuary Act of 1978, declaring the state a manatee refuge and sanctuary. This act and its amendments gave the Florida Department of Environmental Protection (FDEP) the lead role in state manatee protection, including the authority to limit boat speeds and activities in areas critical to manatees, such as zones through warm-water winter-gathering sites.

Effective manatee conservation in Florida requires the cooperation of various state and federal agencies, private organizations, and individuals. Key organizations and agencies involved are the U.S. Fish and Wildlife Service, Marine Mammal Commission, Sirenia Project, Florida Department of Environmental Protection, Georgia Department of Natural Resources, and Save the Manatee Club. Under the umbrella of FDEP, research is directed by the Marine Mammals Team of the Florida Marine Research Institute in St. Petersburg, and management is coordinated by the Bureau of Protected Species Management in Tallahassee. The Florida Marine Patrol (a division of FDEP) handles law enforcement. The Florida Game and Fresh Water Fish Commission, Florida Power & Light Company, Florida Power, and Florida Audubon Society, as well as marine research and rescue facilities including Mote Marine Laboratory, Miami Seaquarium, SeaWorld, and Lowry Park Zoo, also provide valuable research and public awareness assistance.

The U.S. Fish and Wildlife Service (USFWS) bears the overall responsibility for shepherding the recovery of the Florida manatee and has developed a Florida Manatee Recovery Plan, as required by the

A dugong swims over a bright sand bottom flanked by golden pilot jacks and sharksuckers off the coast of Australia.

ESA. The initial plan, developed in 1980, has undergone several revisions. In the latest revision, the USFWS delegated 126 tasks to cooperating agencies and organizations. These tasks fall into several categories, including habitat acquisition, education, law enforcement, research, permit reviews, and information-gathering.

The recovery plan's ultimate goal is to downlist and eventually de-list the Florida manatee. Their 1997 annual report explains that before manatees can be down-listed from endangered to threatened, their populations need to grow or stabilize, their deaths need to be stable at or decreasing from acceptable levels, their habitat must be secure, and threats must be controlled or decreasing. According to the report, habitat loss and watercraft collisions are the greatest threats to manatee recovery in Florida. Manatees along the Atlantic and southwest Florida coasts are at the greatest risk, primarily because of human-related threats; the risk of

A Florida manatee pauses at the boundary of a manatee sanctuary in the Crystal River National Wildlife Refuge. Manatee sanctuaries are closed to boats and swimmers.

another catastrophic red tide also threatens the southwest Florida coast population.

Protection of Dugongs in Australia

Dugongs are legally protected from intentional killing in Australia, except for a harvest by certain indigenous peoples. Dugong management in the Great Barrier Reef region relies on a close working arrangement between the Great Barrier Reef Marine Park Authority, the Queensland Environmental Protection Agency, the Queensland Department of Primary Industries, the Queensland Fisheries Management Authority, and stakeholder groups including local government, indigenous peoples, commercial and recreational fishermen, conservation groups, and local communities.

Within the Great Barrier Reef Marine Park, the dugong harvest is controlled with a permit system, allocated through a Council of Elders that represents the interests of Aboriginal and Torres Strait Islanders communities. The harvest is regulated with consideration for community requirements of dugongs for ceremonial occasions, including weddings, births, and deaths. "Preservation Zones" are designated in which even traditional hunting is not permitted. An 80 percent decline in the dugong population in a large area of the Great Barrier Reef region has prompted most indigenous groups to agree not to hunt along the urban coast of the region. Traditional hunting of dugongs is no longer permitted in southern parts of the region. The Darumbal-Noolar Murree Aboriginal Corporation for Land and Culture of Rockhampton have signed a formal agreement with the Great Barrier Reef Marine Park Authority, agreeing that it would be inappropriate for indigenous hunting to occur in the Great Barrier Reef Marine Park within the Shoalwater Bay Military Training Area.

However, traditional hunting is apparently unregulated in the Torres Strait Protection Zone, an area within which Australia and New Guinea exercise sovereign rights for marine life, including the traditional dugong fishery. Management objectives for a dugong fishery that are mutually agreeable to Torres Strait Islanders and the government are sorely needed for dugongs to survive in this region.

In 1992, the Queensland Shark Control Program responded to the decline of the dugong population by changing its shoreline protection methods. In the Great Barrier Reef region, baited hooks

A Florida manatee swims at the Homosassa Springs State Wildlife Park, where recovering manatees are reacclimated to other manatees and a semi-wild environment.

have replaced shark nets along most beaches to reduce the bycatch of dugongs.

A controversial chain of dugong protection areas (DPAs) has been established to reduce the deaths in commercial gill nets in the southern part of the Great Barrier Reef Marine Park. The areas in which gill nets have been completely banned are called Zone As; the areas in which gill-netting activity has been modified are called Zone Bs. According to Helene Marsh, the 958 square miles (2,395 km²) that include six Zone A areas support 55 percent of the dugongs in the southern Great Barrier Reef region, while the 894 square miles (2,235 km²) that include the eight Zone B areas support 13 percent of the dugongs in this region. Commercial gill-netting has also been modified in Hervey Bay, which once again supports a sizable number of dugongs. The closures have been accompanied by a proportional reduction in the number of commercial fishers allowed to gill net in the area and affected fishers have received almost $4 million in compensation. Many conservationists claim the DPAs are inadequate to prevent dugong mortality and contend that commercial nets do not belong in a sanctuary at all.

As with manatees and all endangered wildlife, habitat protection must be a primary consideration in dugong conservation. According to Helene Marsh, "the greatest challenge ahead will be to ensure the conservation of inshore seagrass beds in the Great Barrier Reef region." This area is plagued by polluted runoff from large agricultural areas and an increasing demand for the development of tourist resorts on islands and the coastline. Only 59 percent of seagrass habitat used by dugongs is protected in the northern half of the Great Barrier Reef, and 72 percent of seagrass meadows in the southern half is protected. In addition to extending protection to more marine habitat, more money and effort need to be targeted toward educating people about the impact of intensive human land use in areas connected hydrologically or otherwise with fragile coastal environments and wildlife. "Experience has shown that it is hard to convince a pro-

spective developer that a resort may have adverse impacts on dugongs and their habitats," writes Marsh. "It will be even harder to convince a farmer that erosion from his property may threaten the survival of sea cows grazing on submarine pastures many kilometers downstream!"

The Road to Recovery

The Florida Manatee Recovery Plan includes four primary objectives:

· Identify and minimize causes of manatee disturbance, injury, and mortality.

· Protect essential habitats.
· Determine and monitor the status of manatee populations and essential habitat.
· Coordinate recovery activities, monitor and evaluate progress, and update/revise the Recovery Plan.

Signs featuring manatees can be found everywhere in Crystal River, Florida.

The causes of manatee disturbance, injury, and mortality in Florida and what must be done to minimize them have been extensively researched and are well understood. Thirteen coastal counties have been identified as "key" to the recovery of the Florida manatee: The counties of Duval, Volusia, Brevard, Indian River, St. Lucie, Martin, Palm Beach, Broward, Dade, Collier, Lee, Sarasota, and Citrus border waters that are frequented by manatees. Research shows these areas have the highest manatee mortality rates, as well as the most significant habitat destruction.

In 1989, the Manatee Protection Bill, which amended the Florida Manatee Sanctuary Act of 1978, directed the FDEP to work with these key coastal counties to improve the condition of the Florida manatee. These counties were asked to designate watercraft speed zones in areas heavily used by manatees. Each county was also asked to develop a comprehensive manatee protection plan (MPP), which would include assessing boating activity patterns, assessing manatee sighting and mortality information, identifying land acquisition projects for manatee protection, and planning a manatee education and awareness program. The key counties have reacted to these directives in a variety of ways.

This aerial view of King Spring in the Crystal River National Wildlife Refuge shows tour boats waiting for manatees to leave a roped-off sanctuary.

ABOVE: *Florida manatees shelter in the warm spring run on a cold winter morning at Blue Spring State Park. A long boardwalk bordering the spring run gives visitors excellent views of manatees in the clear water.*

RIGHT: *Manatees living in salt water are attracted to any source of fresh water and in Florida canals will park beneath running hoses and drink gallons of water. Unfortunately, fresh hose water tempts them to spend more time around docks and marinas, where they are susceptible to being injured by boats.*

Only three counties (Dade, Citrus, and Collier) have adopted their MPP. And, although all but Lee county have agreed to speed limits in manatee zones, the levels set by some counties are too high and inadequate to protect manatees.

Most scientists agree that habitat loss is the most critical fish and wildlife problem in the United States today. The human population in Florida is expected to reach 15 million by 2000. Urbanized land expanded from 0.7 million acres in 1936 to 4.6 million acres in 1994—a 650 percent increase. Approximately 900 people move into the state each day. Perhaps 80 percent settle within six or so miles (16 km) of the coast, where boating is a major recreational activity.

In Tampa Bay on Florida's west coast, 81 percent of the seagrasses and 44 percent of the mangroves and tidal marshes have been destroyed. Charlotte Harbor, also on the west coast and significantly less developed than Tampa Bay, has lost 23 percent of its original wetlands, including 22 percent of its seagrasses and 51 percent of its salt marshes. These quickly disappearing wetlands are important habitat for the Florida manatee and other wildlife.

In their book *Manatees and Dugongs,* Drs. John Reynolds and Dan Odell contend that several conservation actions—all politically unpopular—taken together would go far toward ensuring suitable manatee habitat in the future. First, federal and state governments would need to acquire extensive stretches of undeveloped waterfront land as an initial step toward establishing a system of sanctuaries and refuges where human activities would be prohibited or minimized. Next, human activities (including building marinas or other boating facilities) would need to be limited in critical manatee areas. Finally, and probably most difficult, say Reynolds and Odell, concrete steps toward planning for, and perhaps curbing, population growth in the state would need to be taken.

In response to the need to acquire critical habitat specifically for manatees, the USFWS in 1983 established the Crystal River National Wildlife Refuge on the west coast of Florida. The refuge encompasses approximately forty-six acres of Kings Bay, which is nourished by numerous warm, freshwater springs and forms the headwaters of the Crystal River. More than 300 manatees congregate in the bay during cold winter weather. The refuge draws more than 90,000 visitors a year, primarily boaters,

snorkelers, and divers who want to get a close look at the manatees gathered in the bay during the winter. Seven manatee sanctuaries—off-limits to humans—are posted with buoys and set up around manatee feeding areas and warm springs. The newest of these sanctuaries was established at Three Sisters Spring after a number of reports of manatee harassment by divers and swimmers. The manatees have flocked to these sanctuaries and seem to know they can rest, feed, and nurse there without being disturbed by curious people.

Refuge staff patrol Kings Bay, educating people about manatees, enforcing boat speed zones and sanctuary restrictions, and watching for incidents of people harassing manatees. Harassment, as defined by the Endangered Species Act, is any activity that causes an animal to change its behavior. With manatees, harassment includes chasing, poking, kicking, grabbing, or attempting to ride an animal. Feeding or giving manatees water may also be considered harassment. A conviction can include a $50,000 fine and/or a year in jail.

Other protected winter areas in Florida include Blue Spring State Park on the upper St. Johns River and various other refuges established near the warmwater outflow from power plants throughout the state.

Research

Modern manatee research traces its beginnings to the work of Joseph Curtis Moore in the late 1940s and 1950s and Daniel S. Hartman in the late 1960s. Research for the Florida Manatee Recovery Plan is conducted primarily by the Sirenia Project, the Florida Marine Research Institute, SeaWorld of Florida, Miami Seaquarium, and Mote Marine Laboratory, as well as by other independent researchers and facilities.

The Sirenia Project, a team of federally funded scientists based in Gainesville, Florida, is at the forefront of long-term research dedicated to the Florida manatee. Its work includes assessing habitat, analyzing population trends, gathering life history information, and studying the behavior of wild Florida manatee. Although the Sirenia Project concentrates its research on the manatee in Florida, it exchanges information with sirenian scientists and conservationists worldwide. In 1997, Sirenia Project scientists, working with the Georgia Department of Natural Resources and FDEP, initiated a study on how manatees respond to the elimination of a regularly used warm-water refuge in northeast Florida. They also initiated a study on manatee population genetics. The Project continues its development of a computerized "Scar Catalog" of manatee sightings and its tracking of manatees tagged on the Atlantic coast with satellite/radio transmitters, among other projects. The Sirenia Project provides invaluable information on manatee population dynamics and habitat requirements, research which allows scientists to potentially improve the future of the Florida manatee.

The Florida Marine Research Institute (FMRI) also contributes significantly to Florida manatee research and conservation efforts. Based in St. Petersburg, Florida, FMRI conducts aerial surveys over manatee habitat in Florida and southeast Georgia to gather data regarding manatee distribution and abundance. In 1997, FMRI began a radio telemetry study of tagged manatees in southwest Florida to track their daily and seasonal movements and establish blood chemistry profiles. Telemetry—the recording of data from a remote source, in this case a radio transmitter attached to a manatee's tail—allows researchers to follow the movements of rehabilitated manatees returned to the wild. FMRI scientists also perform necropsies on recovered

manatee carcasses to determine cause of death, a grim task that is fundamental to determining the success of protection measures and identifying new solutions to reduce manatee mortality.

The information FMRI gleans through its aerial surveys, telemetry studies, and necropsies is compiled in their Manatee Geographic Information System (GIS), a computer-based mapping system. This system allows wildlife managers to combine numerical data, such as mortality statistics and regional population numbers, with pictorial data, such as where manatees live and migrate, where carcasses have been recovered, boat traffic patterns, seagrass distribution, proposed development sites, and locations of marinas and boat ramps. The Manatee GIS, which presents a vast quantity of valuable information, helps FMRI scientists to estimate trends in manatee populations and wildlife managers to gain insight into manatees and their environment.

To deal with the problem of manatees being killed in flood control structures and navigation locks, the FDEP has coordinated with the South Florida Water Management District and the Army Corps of Engineers. A promising technological solution is a manatee protection device designed for the wide vertical lift gates that are raised and lowered to manage water level. The device, which consists of strips of piezoelectric film imbedded in tough blocks of polyurethane placed on either side of the lift gate, responds to even the lightest touch of a manatee or other solid living object, but is not triggered by inanimate debris. Unlike former protection devices, this one does not have moving parts that can jam or corrode. It has caused no significant problems on the two gates on which it was installed. Another new device has been developed for water control structures fitted with swinging gates. This device uses closely spaced sets of acoustic beams. When an object passes through the gap between the gates, the beams' signal is interrupted, and the gates are prevented from lowering or closing. Both devices are being tested on coastal structures in south Florida, where the most structure-related manatee mortalities have occurred.

Rescue and Rehabilitation

Over the past five years, between twenty-five and fifty manatees in distress have been rescued annually. In 1997, rescue crews aided nine manatees

This Florida manatee at Blue Spring State Park is tagged with a radio collar on its tail. The transmitters also allow researchers to monitor the movements of manatees released after rehabilitation to ensure they are making a smooth transition to life in the wild.

TOP: *Biologist Bob Bonde from the Sirenia Project records scar patterns to identify individual Florida manatees.*
BOTTOM: *Manatees gather in the warm-water discharge from a power plant at Riviera Beach, Florida. Photograph ©*
Patrick O'Neill/Innerspace Visions.

ABOVE: *An animal care staffer at SeaWorld of Florida adjusts a special wetsuit on an injured manatee calf. The wetsuit is designed to provide flotation and retain body heat.*
RIGHT: *Torres Strait Islanders secure a dugong they have killed. Traditional hunting of dugongs continues in the Torres Strait without governmental regulation. Photograph © Ben Cropp Productions/Innerspace Visions*

struck by watercraft, eight orphaned calves, eight manatees trapped in storm drains and water intake structures, seven tangled in fishing gear, and three suffering from cold-related stress.

In a typical rescue situation, an individual reports an injured manatee to the Florida Marine Patrol on their toll-free hot line (1-800-DIAL FMP, *FMP on a cellular phone, or VHF Channel 16 on marine radio). An officer is dispatched to the scene and, if the manatee is truly injured, a veterinarian and rescue crew are called. Depending on location, the crew may consist of personnel from SeaWorld, Miami Seaquarium, Lowry Park Zoo, Mote Marine Laboratory, Amber Lake Wildlife and Rescue Center, FDEP, and USFWS, among others. When the crew arrives, the animal is captured and its condition evaluated. If possible, it is treated and released. In more serious cases, the manatee is transported to SeaWorld, Lowry Park Zoo, or Miami Seaquarium—the state's three "critical care" facilities. These facilities have medical equipment and staff to care for injured, sick, and orphaned manatees. Beginning in 1997, a few manatees that are generally healthy, but not yet ready for release into the wild, have been transferred to SeaWorld at San Diego, the Columbus Zoo, and the Cincinnati Zoo to make room at the Florida facilities for critically injured manatees.

Manatees whose health has stabilized are transferred to a long-term-care or "soft-release" facility, such as Homosassa Springs State Wildlife Park, where the animals are reacclimated to other manatees and a semiwild environment before being released. The USFWS decides when to release a manatee back into its home waters, based on recommendations by veterinarians and critical care staff. Researchers mark with a PIT (Passive Integrated Transponder) tag, freeze-brand, and/or photograph manatees for future identification before they are released. Some are fitted with a satellite transmitter. These measures allow researchers to track the movements of rehabilitated manatees and find them again should they require medical attention or encounter a dangerous situation. In the past, rehabilitated manatees have attempted to migrate solo to Cuba and the Dry Tortugas—both outside the usual range of Florida manatees—or failed to find warm water during a winter cold snap. In these cases, researchers were able to capture the endangered manatees and return them to a safe environ-ment.

In 1997, of the thirty-five manatees rescued, eight were treated and released on site. Of the twenty-seven that were brought to rehabilitation facilities, fifteen did not survive, seven continue to receive treatment, and five were successfully returned to the wild. Rescue costs run about two million dollars a year, or $30,000 per animal, and include money spent on rescue operations, medical care, and care for captive and rehabilitating manatees. Except for $400,000 from the Save the Manatee Trust Fund, the rehabilitation facilities provide the funding for the rescue efforts. Much of the trust fund money is derived from proceeds of the "Save the Manatee" license tag, one of the more than fifty special license plates in Florida from which a portion of the license fee benefits a particular fund, such as manatee, sea turtle, or panther research.

Law Enforcement

Without adequate law enforcement, regulations protecting manatees are useless. The USFWS and Florida Marine Patrol are the primary agencies responsible for enforcing manatee protection laws in Florida. USFWS officers concentrate their activities in National Wildlife Refuges, enforcing watercraft speed limits in posted manatee zones. Florida Park Service Rangers have jurisdiction regarding manatees living in state park waters, and rangers in national parks, such as Everglades National Park, are able to handle enforcement problems regarding manatees within national park boundaries.

The Florida Marine Patrol has 300 law enforcement officers statewide, a number insufficient to cover Florida's estimated 1,350 miles of coastline and police the more than one million registered boats on the water. During 1997, Florida Marine Patrol officers issued citations for more than 1,600 manatee speed zone violations. Citations issued for violations in Brevard, Dade, Duval, Volusia, and Lee—all "key" counties—accounted for almost 70 percent of those issued.

Studies and polls have indicated that most people support manatee zones and don't mind slowing down to reduce the chance of injuring a manatee. But not everyone complies. In the summer of 1997, the USFWS conducted a six-week manatee speed zone enforcement operation in Brevard County. The operation focused on speed zones in the Banana River, the Indian River, and the Barge

Canal—areas with the highest manatee mortality in the state. A total of 304 speeding tickets was issued, of which 64 percent involved Brevard County residents and nearly 34 percent involved personal watercraft. Most offenders were men in their forties.

Mote Marine Laboratory recently completed a year-long evaluation of boater compliance with speed zone regulations in Sarasota County. The study indicated that an average of 60 percent of boaters complied with posted speed regulations, although compliance was highly variable from one area to the next. The study also found that operators of personal watercraft were the least compliant, with an average of only 36 percent obeying posted speeds. The presence of law enforcement increased the level of boater compliance significantly.

The findings of the Brevard and Sarasota County evaluations serve as a reminder that although public opinion generally sways toward the preservation of the manatee, many people who are actually out on the water ignore manatee speed zones. The Sarasota study recommends the alloca-

A manatee mailbox on Highway 19 near Crystal River, Florida.

tion of additional funds, personnel, and resources for law enforcement activities throughout Florida.

Education and Advocacy

Education forms a major component of the manatee protection and recovery effort. Information about Florida manatees is widespread throughout the state; it is difficult to go anywhere on the coast without learning something about manatees. Children study them in school, signs are posted in parks and by boat ramps near manatee habitats, and aquariums such as SeaWorld of Florida, Miami Seaquarium, and The Living Seas at Walt Disney World offer educational manatee programs. Both Homosassa Springs and Blue Spring State Park offer excellent manatee programs, and during the winter, Blue Spring is one of the best places to observe—from an elevated boardwalk—up to 100 wild manatees gathering in the clear, warm water.

In 1997, a Manatee Education Center was opened at the entrance to Homosassa Springs State Wildlife Park in the Crystal River National Wildlife Refuge. Through the center, schools, chambers of commerce, and other outlets, the refuge provides educational outreach, such as a video on proper manatee-watching etiquette; this video is distributed to dive shops that conduct underwater dive training and provide manatee tours in the Crystal River area.

Funded by the USFWS in cooperation with the FDEP, the center is one of many programs on which FDEP expends considerable effort and money to educate people about manatee conservation. The Bureau of Protected Species Management recently produced new manatee behavior posters, as well as a manatee travel activity sheet for families visiting coastal areas. Outreach staff respond to information requests and provide an Internet site (see Appendix III). The Florida Marine Research Institute developed six educational presentations on manatee topics for distribution to selected United States schools; additionally, FMRI provides educational displays, handles requests for manatee information, and maintains its Internet site (see Appendix III) with current manatee information and recent data. Founded by singer/songwriter Jimmy Buffet and U.S. Senator Bob Graham in 1982, the Save the Manatee Club (SMC) is the principal grassroots manatee advocate in the country. The club's stated purpose is to promote public awareness and educa-

ABOVE: *The back of this manatee has been extensively mutilated by repeated boat strikes.*

LEFT: *This sign posted in Crystal River, Florida, signals boaters to idle through this area or face fines if caught speeding. Because approximately 1.1 million boats—or about 400 boats to every manatee—ply Florida's waterways at any given time, it is important for boaters to look out for manatees and obey posted speeds.*

tion; to sponsor research, rescue, and rehabilitation efforts; and to advocate and take appropriate legal action when manatees' interests are threatened. A nonprofit organization that boasts more than 40,000 members, SMC is one of the most important manatee education providers in the United States.

Among its many services, SMC provides free manatee education packets and staff interviews for students; an educator's guide, four-color poster, coloring and activity book, and free in-service programs for educators; volunteer speakers to schools and civic groups in Florida and select areas across the United States; and equipment for educational manatee programs, such as the Blue Spring State Park's manatee interpretive program. An educational manatee video was produced by SMC and the Florida Advisory Council on Environmental Education and is distributed without charge to schools throughout Florida. In cooperation with USFWS and the Professional Association of Diving Instructors, SMC printed and distributed 40,000 "If You Love Me, Don't Disturb Me" pamphlets designed for swim-with-the-manatee programs. The club also prints and distributes thousands of public awareness signs and stickers for shoreline property owners and boaters.

As manatee advocates, SMC staff review plans, make recommendations, and lobby to implement manatee protection in Florida's key manatee counties. The club also files legal challenges against development projects that may harm manatees and their habitat. In 1997, SMC staff helped prevent a casino cruise ship from using a marina on the Crystal River as a point of departure; the ship caused documented destruction of river bottom habitat and posed a threat to manatees wintering in the river. If a boat speed limit is challenged by a county, SMC intervenes on the state's behalf, and the club challenges state laws that are not strong enough to ensure adequate manatee protection.

The investment of time, money, and resources that has been infused—and continues to be infused—into sirenian conservation by government, private organizations, and caring individuals is a tremendous worldwide effort. But we must continue to learn about sirenians and their survival needs; we must support the development and *enforcement* of strict conservation laws protecting them and other vulnerable wildlife; and we must maintain habitat sirenians need to thrive over the next millennium and beyond. Some of the actions we can each take to protect sirenians are ridiculously simple. For instance, we can slow our boats in manatee zones and refrain from feeding them when they nose up to a dock. These are small but critical steps. Other actions, such as developing a workable plan to curb the explosive growth of the human population and finding ways to live from the earth without damaging it, will require no small amount of resolve and sacrifice. But these, too, demand our immediate attention.

People have been telling stories about sirenians for thousands of years. The classical legends of mermaids and sirens and the myths of manatees and dugongs recounted by indigenous cultures provide vital clues to our history as humans and how we view our world. As we look to a new millennium, we are faced with important choices. Do we arrogantly continue our perceived dominion over the planet by developing its wild lands, eliminating other species, and reproducing without consideration for dwindling resources or future generations' welfare? Or do we look deep within ourselves and thumb through the pages of our own storied history to relearn how to coexist with all living things—knowledge we once held close, but now have largely forgotten.

Right now, we are writing the stories that will

Manatees rarely get respite from the throngs of eager snorkelers who invade the warm-water springs in winter to swim with these large, gentle animals.

A Florida manatee approaches a photographer for a scratch near Crystal River.

be told of us by coming generations. Two centuries from now, will our descendants describe how we crushed the sirenians with boats, entangled them in debris, and destroyed their habitat until none were left? Or will they recount how we slowed our boats where manatees played, protected valuable habitat, and kept garbage and toxins out of the environment? Will they tell of how we rekindled a reverence for our home planet and all its wondrous inhabitants?

We now have our chance to ensure manatees and dugongs remain a living part of our legacy and do not meet the sad, unalterable fate of the Steller's sea cow. We know well what must be done. What better time to write a story of reverence and preservation, one that will be retold many times in the centuries to follow.

A B O V E : *A Florida manatee enjoys a back rub from an underwater photographer near Crystal River.*
L E F T : *Manatees linger at the bottom of the spring run at Blue Spring State Park, Florida.*

Guidelines for Protecting Manatees

THE FOLLOWING ARE guidelines established through the cooperative effort of the Save the Manatee Club, Florida Power & Light Company, U.S. Fish and Wildlife Service, and Florida Department of Environmental Protection (Office of Protected Species Management).

Please follow these guidelines to ensure the safety of manatees when swimming or boating near them.

1. Being Near Manatees

· Look, but don't touch manatees. Also, don't feed manatees or give them water. If manatees become accustomed to being around people, this can alter their behavior in the wild, perhaps causing them to lose their natural fear of boats and humans, and this may make them more susceptible to harm. *Passive observation* is the best way to interact with manatees and all wildlife.

· Do not pursue or chase a manatee while you are swimming, snorkeling, diving, or operating a boat.

· Never poke, prod, or stab a manatee with your hands, feet, or any object.

· If a manatee avoids you, you should avoid it.

· Don't isolate or single out an individual manatee from its group, and don't separate a cow from her calf.

· Don't attempt to snag, hook, hold, grab, pinch, or ride a manatee.

· Avoid excessive noise and splashing if a manatee appears in your swimming area.

· Use snorkel gear when attempting to watch manatees. The sound of bubbles from SCUBA gear may cause manatees to leave the area.

· When snorkeling, don't wear a weight belt. Float at the surface of the water and passively observe the manatee. Look, but don't touch.

2. Don't Enter Areas Designated as "No Entry Manatee Refuge"

These areas have been identified by the Florida Department of Environmental Protection and the U.S. Fish and Wildlife Service as crucial for manatee survival.

3. When Boating or Jet Skiing

· Abide by the posted speed zone signs while in areas known to have manatees present or when observations indicate manatees might be present. Observations may include seeing a swirl at the surface caused by the manatee when diving; seeing the animal's back, snout, tail, or flipper break the surface of the water; or hearing it when it surfaces to breathe.

The underwater observatory at Homosassa Springs State Wildlife Park offers excellent views of manatees in their natural environment.

· Wear polarized sunglasses to reduce glare on the surface of the water. This will enable you to see manatees more easily.

· Try to stay in deep-water channels. Manatees can be found in shallow, slow-moving rivers, estuaries, lagoons, and coastal areas. Avoid boating over seagrass beds and shallow areas.

· Remain at least 50 feet away from a manatee when operating a powerboat. Don't operate a boat near large concentrations of manatees.

· If you like to water ski, please choose areas that manatees do not use, or cannot enter, such as land-locked lakes.

· Please don't discard monofilament line, hooks, or any other litter into the water. Manatees may ingest or become entangled in this debris and can become injured or even die. Note: discarding monofilament fishing line into the waters of Florida is unlawful.

Remember, to report manatee injuries, deaths, tag sightings, or harassment, call the Florida Marine Patrol at 1-800-DIAL FMP (1-800-342-5367).

Manatee Area Signs

Idle Speed Zone—a zone in which boats are not permitted to go any faster than necessary to be steered.

Caution area—an area frequently inhabited by manatees, requiring caution on the part of boaters to avoid disturbing or injuring the animals.

Resume Normal Safe Operation—a sign indicating that you may resume safe boating speed; visible as you leave a protected area.

No Entry Zone—a protected zone that prohibits boating, swimming, and diving for the protection of manatees.

Slow Speed Zone—a minimum-wake zone where boats must not be on a plane and must be level in the water.

Two Florida manatees. The animal on the right has been returned to the wild after being in captivity, as indicated by the number freeze branded onto its side.

Organizations Involved in Manatee and Dugong Conservation

Manatees

Amber Lake Wildlife Rescue and Rehabilitation
Center
297 Artists Ave.
Englewood, FL 34223
(941) 475-4585

Blue Spring State Park
2100 West French Ave.
Orange City, FL 32763
(904) 775-3663
www.dep.state.fl.us/parks/BlueSpring/
bluespring.html

Crystal River and Chassahowitzka National Wildlife Refuges
1502 S.E. Kings Bay Drive
Crystal River, FL 34429
(352) 563-2088
www.gorp.com/gorp/resource/us_nwr/
fl_cryst.htm

Dolphin Research Center
P.O. Box 522875
Marathon Shores, FL 33052
(305) 289-1121
www.dolphins.org

Florida Marine Research Institute
Florida Department of Environmental Protection
100 Eighth Avenue, S.E.
St. Petersburg, FL 33701-5095
(727) 896-8626
www.fmri.usf.edu

Florida Power & Light Company
Environmental Services Department
P.O. Box 14000
Juno Beach, FL 33408
1-800-552-8440

Georgia Department of Natural Resources
Nongame and Endangered Wildlife Program
One Conservation Way
Brunswick, GA 31523
(912) 264-7218
www.dnr.state.ga.us/dnr/wild

Homosassa Springs State Wildlife Park
4150 South Suncoast Blvd.
Homasassa, FL 34446
(352) 628–2311
www.citrusdirectory.com\hsswp

Lowry Park Zoo
7530 North Boulevard

Tampa, FL 33604
(813) 935-8552

Miami Seaquarium
4400 Rickenbacker Causeway
Miami, FL 33149
(305) 361-5705
www.miamiseaquarium.com

Save the Manatee Club
500 N. Maitland Ave.
Maitland, FL 32751
(800) 432-JOIN
www.savethemanatee.org

SeaWorld of Florida
7007 SeaWorld Drive
Orlando, FL 32809
(407) 351-3600
www.4adventure.com

The Sirenia Project
U.S. Geological Survey
412 N.E. 16th Avenue, Rm. 250
Gainesville, FL 32601-3701
(352) 372-2571
www.fcsc.usgs.gov/sirenia

Dugongs

Australian Nature Conservation Agency
GPO Box 636
Belconnen, ACT
2617 Australia
(06) 250 0200
www.anbg.gov.au/anca/anca.html

Conservation Commission of the
Northern Territories
P.O. Box 496
Palmerston, NT
0831 Australia
PHONE: 250 0200
www.atn.com.au/parks/ntparks.html

Department of Conservation and
Land Management
Hackett Drive
Crawley, WA

6009 Australia
(08) 9442 0300
www.calm.wa.gov.au

NSW National Parks and Wildlife Service
P.O. Box 1967
Hurtsville, NSW
2220 Australia
1 300 36 1967 or (02) 9585 6333

The Department of Tropical Environment Studies
and Geography
James Cook University of North Queensland
Townsville, Queensland
4811 Australia
(77) 81 4761/4521

The Great Barrier Reef Marine Park Authority
P.O. Box 1379
Townsville, Queensland
4810 Australia
(077) 500 700
www.gbrmpa.gov.au

The Queensland Department of Environment
and Heritage
160 Ann Street
P.O. Box 155
Brisbane Albert Street, QLD
4002 Australia
(07) 3227 7111
www.env.qld.gov.au

Bibliography

Ackerman, Bruce et al. "Trends and Patterns in Mortality of Manatees in Florida 1974–1992." In: *Population Biology of the Florida Manatee, Information and Technology Report 1*. National Biological Service, Department of the Interior, 1995.

———. "The Behavior of the Dugong (Dugong dugon) in Relation to Conservation and Management." *Bulletin of Marine Science*, 31(3): 1981.

———. "Suckling in *Dugong dugon*." *Journal of Mammalogy*, 65(3): 1984.

Anderson, Paul K. "Dugong Behavior and Ecology." *The Explorers Journal*, 64(4): December 1986.

———. "Shark Bay Dugongs in Summer. I." *Behaviour*, 134: 1996.

Anonymous. Manatees and Boats. *Mote News*, (Mote Marine Laborary, Sarasota) 41(3): 1996.

Baughman, J.L. "Some Early Notices on American Manatees and the Mode of Their Capture." *Journal of Mammalogy*, 27(3): 1946.

Beck, Cathy A. and Nélio B. Barros. "The Impact of Debris on the Florida Manatee." *Marine Pollution Bulletin*, 22(10): 1991.

Best, Robin C. "Apparent Dry-Season Fasting in Amazonian Manatee (Mammalia: Sirenia)." *Biotropica*, 15(1): 1983.

Bradley, Richard et al. "The Pre-Columbian Exploitation of the Manatee in Mesoamerica." *University of Oklahoma Department of Anthropology, Papers in Anthropology*, 24(1): 1983.

Bryden, Michael et al. *Dugongs, Whales, Dolphins, and Seals: A Guide to the Sea Mammals of Australasia*. St. Leonards: Allen & Unwin, 1998.

Cumbaa, Stephen L. "Aboriginal Use of Marine Mammals in the Southeastern United States." *Southeastern Archaeological Conference Bulletin* 17: 1980.

Deutsch, Charles J. et al. "Radio-Tracking Manatees from Land and Space." *MTS Journal*, 32(1): 1998.

Dollman, Guy. "Dugongs from Mafia Island and a Manatee from Nigeria." *Natural History Magazine* (London), 4(28): 1933.

———. "Manatees of the Amazon." *Sea Frontiers*, 27(1): 1981.

Domning, Daryl P. "Commercial Exploitation of Manatees *Trichechus* in Brazil c. 1785-1973." *Biological Conservation*, 22(2): 1982.

———. "Evolution of Manatees." *Journal of Paleontology*, 56(3): 1982.

———. "West Indian Tuskers." *Natural History*, 103(4): April 1994.

———. "1997 Florida Manatee Mortality." *Sirenews*, No. 29, April 1998.

Eliot, T.S. "The Love Song of J. Alfred Prufrock." From *Collected Poems 1909–1962*. Harcourt Brace Jovanovich, 1963.

Gallivan, G. James et al. "Temperature Regulation in the Amazonian Manatee (*Trichechus inunguis*)." *Physiological Zoology*, 56(2): 1983.

Gilmore, Raymond M. "Fauna and Ethnozoology." In: Julian H. Steward (ed.), *Handbook of South American Indians*, Vol. 6. New York, Cooper Square Publishers, Inc., 1963.

Grigione, M.M. "Observations on the Status and Distribution of the West African Manatee in Cameroon." *African Journal of Ecology*, 34(2): 1996.

Hudson, Bridget E.T. "Dugongs." *Wildlife in Papua New Guinea*, 77/16: 1977.

Humboldt, Alexander von. *Voyage aux régions équinoxiales du Nouveau Continent, fait en 1799,*

A mangrove snapper shelters under a Florida manatee, Crystal River.

1800, 1801, 1802, 1803 et 1804, par Al. de Humboldt et A. Bonpland. . . . Tome second. English Edition, 1852–53.

Jones, Santhabpan. "The Dugong or the So-Called Mermaid, *Dugong dugon* (Müller) of the Indo-Sri Lanka Waters." *Spolia Zeylanica*, 35(I–II): 1981.

Kingdon, Jonathan. *East African Mammals: An Atlas of Evolution in Africa.* Vol. 1. London and New York, Academic Press, 1971.

Lefebvre, Lynn W. and James A. Powell, Jr. *Manatee Grazing Impacts on Seagrasses in Hobe Sound and Jupiter Sound in Southeast Florida During the Winter of 1988–89.* NTIS Document No. PB 90-271883: vi +36, 1990.

Loveland, Franklin O. "Tapirs and Manatees." In: M.W. Helms & F.O. Loveland (eds.), *Frontier Adaptations in Lower Central America.* Philadelphia, Inst. for Study of Human Issues, 1976.

Marden, Luis. "Guatemala Revisited." *National Geographic*, 92(4): 1947.

Marmontel, Miriam et al. "Population Viability Analysis of the Florida Manatee (*Trichechus manatus latirostris*), 1976–1991." *Conservation Biology*, 11(2): 1997.

Marsh, Helene. "An Ecological Basis for Dugong Conservation in Australia." In: M.L. Augee (ed.), *Marine Mammals of Australasia: Field Biology and Captive Management.* Sydney: Royal Zoological Society of New South Wales, 1988.

———. "Tropical Siren." *Australian Geographic*, 21: January–March 1991.

———. "Going, Going, Dugong." *Nature Australia*, Winter 1997.

Marsh, Helene, P.J. Corkeron, I. Lawler, J.M. Lanyon and A.R. Preen. "The Status of Dugongs in the Great Barrier Reef Region, South of Cape Bedford." *Great Barrier Reef Marine Park Authority Research Publication No. 41*: 1996.

Marsh, Helene et al. "Present-Day Hunting and Distribution of Dugongs in the Wellesyle Islands (Queensland)." *Biological Conservation*, 19: 1980–81.

Marsh, Helene et al. *Status of the Dugong in the Torres Strait Area: Results of an Aerial Survey in the Perspective of Information on Dugong Life History and Current Catch Levels.* Report to Australian National Parks & Wildlife Services, 1984.

Marsh, Helene et al. "The Distribution and Abundance of the Dugong in Shark Bay, Western Australia." *Wildlife Research*, 21(1): 1994.

Marsh, Helene et al. "Can Dugongs Survive in Palau?" *Biological Conservation*, 72: 1995.

Marsh, Helene et al. "The Sustainability of the Indigenous Dugong Fishery in Torres Strait, Australia/Papua New Guinea." *Conservation Biology*, 11(6): 1997.

McKillop, Heather I. "Prehistoric Exploitation of the Manatee in the Maya and Circum-Caribbean Areas." *World Archaeology*, 16(3): 1985.

Nietschmann, Bernard. "Hunting and Ecology of Dugongs and Green Turtles, Torres Strait, Australia." *National Geographic Society Research Report*, 17: 1984.

Nietschmann, Bernard and Judith. "Good Dugong, Bad Dugong; Bad Turtle, Good Turtle." *Natural History*, 90(5): 1981.

O'Shea, Thomas J. et al. "Distribution, Status, and Traditional Significance of the West Indian Manatee *Trichechus manatus* in Venezuela." *Biological Conservation*, 46: 1988.

Pain, Stephanie. "Where Manatees May Safely Swim." *New Scientist*, No. 2039: July 20, 1996.

Parer-Cook, Elizabeth and David Parer. "The Case of the Vanishing Mermaids." *Geo*, 12(3): 1990.

Powell, James A. Jr. "Evidence of Carnivory in Manatees (*Trichechus manatus*)." *Journal of Mammalogy*, 59(2): 1978.

Preen, Anthony. "Diet of Dugongs." *Journal of Mammalogy*, 76(1): 1995.

———. "Impacts of Dugong Foraging on Seagrass Habitats." *Marine Ecology Progress Series*, Vol. 124: 1995.

Preen, Anthony and Helene Marsh. "Response of Dugongs to Large-scale Loss of Seagrass from Hervey Bay, Queensland, Australia." *Wildlife Research*, 22(4): 1995.

Pritchard, Peter C.H. and Herbert W. Kale. *Saving What's Left.* Maitland, Florida Audubon Society, 1994.

Quammen, David. *The Song of the Dodo: Island Biogeography in an Age of Extinctions.* New York: Scribner, 1996.

Reynolds, John E., III and Daniel K. Odell. *Manatees and Dugongs.* New York: Facts on File, 1992.

Rosas, Fernando César Weber. "Biology, Conservation and Status of the Amazonian Manatee *Trichechus inunguis.*" *Mammal Review*, 24(2):

1994.

Rouse, Irving. "The Arawak." In: Julian H. Steward (ed.), *Handbook of South American Indians*, Vol. 4. New York, Cooper Square Publishers, Inc., 1963.

Seifert, Douglas David. "The Sirenian's Final Aria, Part Two" *Ocean Realm*, Summer 1996.

Shankland, Jessie. "Predation of Dugong by Tiger Sharks—Shark Bay." Notes from James Scheerer Research Charter, July 1997.

Sikes, Sylvia. "How to Save the Mermaids." *Oryx*, 12(4): 1975.

Simpson, George Gaylord. "Sea Sirens." *Natural History*, 30(1): 1930.

———. "Some Carib Indian Mammal Names." *American Museum Novit.*, No. 1119: 1941.

Smith, Kenneth N. *Manatee Habitat and Human-Related Threats to Seagrass in Florida: A Review*. Tallahassee, Florida Department of Environmental Protection: 38 pp., 1993.

Smith, Nigel J.H. "Caimans, Capybaras, Otters, Manatees, and Man in Amazonia." *Biological Conservation*, 19(3): 1981.

Solov, Dean. "Researchers Discover Butchered Manatees." *Tampa Tribune*, September 28, 1995.

Steller, Georg Wilhelm. *Journal of a Voyage with Bering 1741–1742*. Edited by O.W. Frost. Translated by Margritt A. Engel and O.W. Frost. Stanford: Stanford University Press, 1988.

Thomson, Donald F. "The Dugong Hunters of Cape York." *Journal of the Royal Anthropology Institute of Great Britain and Ireland*, 64: 1934.

Timm, Robert M. et al. "Ecology, Distribution, Harvest, and Conservation of the Amazonian Manatee (*Trichechus inunguis*) in Ecuador." *Biotropica*, 18(2): 1986.

U.S. Fish and Wildlife Service. *Florida Manatee Recovery Accomplishments, 1997 Annual Report*. Jacksonville, FL., 1998.

Van Meter, Victoria. *The West Indian Manatee in Florida*. Juno Beach: Florida Power & Light Company, 1987.

Wells, Randy. "New State-Funded Manatee Research at Mote." *Mote News*, (Mote Marine Laborary, Sarasota) 42(3): 1997.

Zeiller, Warren. *Introducing the Manatee*. Gainesville: University Press of Florida, 1992.

Index

About the Author and Photographer

Jeff Ripple, natural history writer and photographer, has devoted nearly fifteen years to exploring and photographing the natural areas of Florida.

His articles and photographs have appeared in publications such as *The New York Times, Outside, BBC Wildlife, Cortlandt Forum, Men's Fitness, Sail, River Magazine, Ocean Realm, Backpacker, Birder's World,* and *Defenders,* among others. Jeff is the author of *Big Cypress Swamp and the Ten Thousand Islands* (University of South Carolina Press, 1992), *The Florida Keys: The Natural Wonders of an Island Paradise* (Voyageur Press, 1995), *Sea Turtles* (Voyageur Press, 1996), *Southwest Florida's Wetland Wilderness* (University Presses of Florida, 1996), and *Florida: The Natural Wonders* (Voyageur Press, 1997). He also edited and contributed to *The Wild Heart of Florida* (University Presses of Florida). He is currently working on a photography project in the Fakahatchee Strand of southwest Florida.

Jeff, his wife Renée, and their cats Tabatha, Suwannee, and Natalie live in a small house in the woods near Gainesville, Florida.

Doug Perrine, freelance photojournalist, has been photographing manatees since 1981. His first published photographs accompanied articles on manatees in *Florida Wildlife & Underwater USA* in 1985. He has since contributed his photographs to hundreds of magazines, including *National Geographic, Smithsonian, Natural History, National/International Wildlife, BBC Wildlife, Time, Newsweek, USNews & World Report,* and *Omni,* as well as books, calendars, posters, and notecards. In 1995, he took first place in the animal behavior category in the Wildlife Photographer of the Year Competition. Doug is the author of *Sharks* (Voyageur Press, 1995), *Mysteries of the Sea* (1997), *Ripley's Whales and Dolphins* (1999), and *Sharks and Rays of the World* (Voyageur Press, 1999).

Doug earned his master's degree in marine biology from the University of Miami and served as a Peace Corps volunteer in Morocco and Micronesia.